a travel kit of northern india

a travel kit of northern india

C.C.S. Menon

Books For All
Delhi

Distributed by :
D.K. Publishers Distributors Pvt. Ltd.
1, Ansari Road,
New Delhi - 110 002
Phs.: 327 8368, 326 1465
Fax: 326 4368
E-mail: dkpd@del3.vsnl.net.in
Web site: www.dkpdindia.com.

First Published : 1999

ISBN : 81-7386-217-6

Published by :
Books For All
B-2, Vardhaman Palace,
Nimri Commercial Centre,
Near Ashok Vihar Phase-IV,
Delhi-110 052
Ph.: 740 1672, Fax: 745 2453
E-mail: lpp@nde.vsnl.net.in
Web site: www.lppindia.com.

Printed at :
D.K. Fine Art Press Pvt. Ltd.
A-6, Nimri Commercial Centre
Near Ashok Vihar Phase-IV,
Delhi-110 052
Ph.: 745 2451, 743 6929
Fax: 745 2453

Printed in India

On First Four Pages
1. An Indian Woman in traditional dress
2. A Sikh family at Red Fort, Delhi
3. Taj Mahal, Agra
4. Ganga River

The Tower of Victory (Vijay Stambh) & a portrait of Maharana Pratap at Chittaurgarh

A Punjabi Woman in traditional dress at Chandigarh

Pilgrims bathing in Ganga river at Haridwar

A Camel cart rider & A Snack vendor at Jaipur

Naina Devi Temple at Kangra

Erotic sculptures at Khajuraho

The valley of Leh

An Bara Imambara &
a Muslim man at Lucknow

A Child on camel cart &
A Musician at Pushkar

An Elephant in joyful mood at Rajaji National Park

A Tiger & a bird
at Sariska Tiger Reserve

A Pilgrim on Ganga ghat(bank of Ganga river) at Varanasi

Contents

INDIA

India is the living example of unity in diversity. A land of spectacular dimensions, India, with her Keleidoscopic attractions offers a variety of feasts to the eyes, music to the ears, tastes to the palates and foods to the faculty of thinking. Independent existence of old traditions and cultures and at the same time interesting examples of the same duly integrated with the modernity have to be seen to be believed.

India's rich natural wealth had been luring foreign traders, and invaders who had left on the country their influences, regionalsed or localised in terms of religions and faith; cultures, languages etc. India's history goes back to the time when Hinduism was founded. Foreign influences over the centuries have resulted in establishment of different religious faiths and today a number of religions co-exist peacefully with **Hinduism** such as Buddhism, Jainism, Christianity, Islam etc.

India covers an area of approximately 33 lakh square kilometres with nearly 100 crores of people. On an average, only 52 per cent of population is literate.

The per capita income of the country is approximately Rs.4,300/- and nearly 30 per cent of the population is below poverty line.

The main religions being followed in the country are Hinduism (83%), Islam (11%), Christianity (3%), and Sikhism (2%).

Wildife: There are 81,251 living species of animals in the country, according to the estimates of the Zoological Survey of India. Following are the major species of wild animals included in the Schedule of the Wildlife (Protection) Act 1972, as rare and endanagered species.

Mammals such as Lion, Caracal, Desert Cat, Marbled Cat, Golden Cat, Snow Leopard, Hispid Hare, Pygmy Hog, Braw-antlered Deer, Musk Deer, Yak, Markhor, Lion-tailed Monkey, Wild Ass, birds such as Jerdon's Courser, White-winged Wood Duck, Forest Spotted Owlet, Tragopan Pheasants, Reptiles such as Gharial, Indian Egg-eating Snake, Leathery Turtle, etc. can be seen in India.

There are 411 wildlife sanctuaries in India. India consists of 25 States and 7 Union Territories.

NORTH INDIA

North India consists of six states such as Haryana, Himachal Pradesh, Jammu & Kashmir, Punjab, Rajasthan and Uttar Pradesh, besides one Union territory of Chandigarh and the National Capital Territory of Delhi.

Delhi

Area	:	1,483, sq.kms.
Population	:	94.21 lakhs
Main Language Groups	:	Hindi (76%), Punjabi (13%), Urdu (6%)
Main Religious Groups	:	Hindus (84%), Muslims (8%), Sikhs (6%)

Climate

The monsoon starts normally from early July and lasts till September and in some years up to October. May and June are the hottest months with a dry climate. December and January are the coldest.

During May and June the maximum temperature shoots up to 40°C. Temperature comes down gradually, from October and after the winter, it starts going up from the month of March.

The best time to visit is between November and March.

Haryana

Area	:	44,212 sq.kms.
Capital	:	Chandigarh
Population	:	164.64 lakhs
Main Language Groups	:	Hindi (88%), Punjabi (9%), and Urdu (2%)
Main Religious Groups	:	Hindu (89%), Sikhs (6%), Muslims (4%)

Climate

The monsoon starts normally from early July and lasts till September and in some years up to October. May and June are the hottest months with a dry climate. December and January are the coldest.

During May and June the maximum temperature shoots up to 40°C. Temperature comes down gradually, from October and after the winter, it starts going up from the month of March.

The best time to visit is between November and March.

Himachal Pradesh

Area	:	55,673 sq.kms.
Capital	:	Shimla
Population	:	51.71 lakhs
Main Language Groups	:	Hindi (88%) Punjabi (6%)
Main Religious Groups	:	Hindus (96%), Muslims (2%)

Climate

The higher mountains of this State are permanently under snow. The summer months of May and June can be very hot and humid at lower altitudes. Rainy season starts from the middle of June and rains continue till October.

The best months to visit the tourist attractions in the State for normal tourists are April, May, June, October and November, whereas for those interested in skiing the best months are January, February and March.

The pleasant summers of this hill state make it a popular summer holiday resort. Besides popular resort towns like Shimla and Kullu-Manali, Himachal has secluded hill retreats like Mashobra, Kufri, Nal dehra, Manikaran, Naggar etc; which are ideal for anglers, trekkers and those wanting a quiet getaway. Adventures in the form of trekking, river rafting, rock-climbing, skiing at Kufri and Manali, hand-gliding, para-gliding and fishing are the special attractions for tourists.

Himachal is famous for Pashmina, Honey, Dry Fruits, Angoori, (Wine) Wooden Handicrafts, Handmade Carpets, Shawls, Caps, Kangra Tea, Silver Jewellery etc.

Jammu & Kashmir

Area	:	2,22,236 sq. kms.
Capital	:	Srinagar (Summer)
		Jammu (Winter)
Population	:	59.87 lakhs
Main Language Groups	:	Kashmiri (52%), Dogri (24%) Hindi (17%), Punjabi (3%)
Main Religious Groups	:	Muslims (64%), Hindus (32%), Sikhs (2%)

Climate

Jammu

The maximum temperature rises above 30°C from April onwards and reaches even 40°C in June where-after it starts coming down gradually. Though maximum rainfall is in the months of June, August and September, occasional rains continue throughout the year.

The best months to visit are November to March.

Kashmir

Minimum temperature goes below O°C from November to January. The maximum temperature does not go above 30°C even in the summer months of May and June. This region gets rains throughout the year though in small quantities.

The best months to visit are March to September.

This state has 15 wildlife sanctuaries. Dachigam Wildlife Sanctuary in the Kashmir Valley is the home of the Hangul or the Kashmir Stag, a species of rare deer.

Punjab

Area	:	50.362 sq.kms.
Capital	:	Chandigarh
Population	:	202.82 lakhs
Main Language Groups	:	Punjabi (84%), Hindi (14%)
Main Religious Groups	:	Sikhs (61%), Hindus (34%)

Climate

The monsoon starts normally from early July and lasts till September and in some years up to October. May and June are the hottest months with a dry climate. December and January are the coldest.

During May and June the maximum temperature shoots up to 40°C. Temperature comes down gradually, from October and after the winter, it starts going up from the month of March.

The best time to visit is between November and March.

Rajasthan

Area	:	3,42,239 sq.kms.
Capital	:	Jaipur
Population	:	440.06 lakhs
Main Language Groups	:	Hindi (90%), Urdu (2%) Punjabi (2%)
Main Religious Groups	:	Hindus (89%), Muslims (7%)

Climate

Except in the hills, particularly around Mt. Abu, the summer temperatures are very high with a maximum of 46°C and an average of 38°C during the summer months.

Rains start from July and continue sporadically up to September, which may extend up to October in some years. December and January are the coldest months.

The best time to visit is between November and March.

Rajasthan has 24 wildlife sancturaies. Ranthambore spread over the Aravalis and Vindhya range is said to have India's friendliest tigers, because they are seen quite often in the day. Keoladeo Ghana Bird Sanctuary in the Bharatpur National Park is the largest water bird sanctuary in India for migratory and residential birds. This is the only place in the whole of South Asia where the Siberian Cranes choose to spend their winter.

Rajasthan is a handicrafts shopper's treasure trove. Diamond studded jewellery in gold and silver, local *Kundan* style jewellery, radiantly emproidered Rajasthani camel leather *majhare* (footware) and other gilt embossed camel hide products, toys, puppets, miniature paintings, marble statuettes, tie-and-dye fabrics, printed textiles, exotic blue pottery & enamel ware, woollen carpets, ruggs etc., are some of the important items.

Uttar Pradesh

Area : 2,94,411sq.kms.

Capital	:	Lucknow
Population	:	1391.12 lakhs
Main Language Groups	:	Hindi (89%), Urdu(10%)
Main Religious Groups	:	Hindus (83%); Muslims (16%)

Climate

Between April and June temperatures are likely to rise quite high and reach even 48°C. Hot dry winds also blow occasionally. Monsoon rains begin in July and sporadic rains continue till middle of October. Eastern U.P. gets more rain-fall than the western side.

The best season to visit is between November and March.

Uttar Pradesh has 22 wildlife sanctuaries with population of tigers, leopards, spotted deer, elephants sloth bear, jungle cat, dhole etc. Agra in U.P. is famous for marble in-lay work, which comes in the form of plates, trays, vases etc. Leather goods of Agra like shoes, jackets, briefcases, handbags etc. have the lowest prices in the country, and are of excellent quality. *Chikan* work fabrics and semiprecious jewellery in the ornate Mughal style are other temptations. Varanasi is famous for silks and brocades, brassware, ivory, gold jewellery and carpets.

Agra

Agra located about 200 Kilometres away from Delhi, had been the capital of the Mughal empire ever since Mughal invaded India. It was here the founder of the dynasty, Babur, laid out the first formal Persian garden on the banks of the River *Yamuna* .

Taj Mahal

Taj Mahal is the most exquisite specimen of human architecture and the most gorgeous romance of wedded love. It is a poem in marble, built in the 17th century by the Mughal Emperor Shah Jahan, in memory of his wife, Empress Mumtaz Mahal.

The Taj Mahal is perfectly proportioned, exquisitely detailed. It comprises a forecourt, a majestic entrance leading to a formal Mughal Garden lined by dark cypresses with the usual water channels and fountains, the mausoleum itself on a high red sandstone base with its domed two-storied building flanked on four sides by tapering minarets; and an attached mosque. The Taj was topped with a gold finial which is missing presently.

White marble and red sandstone, silver and gold, Carnelian and Jasper, monostone laid lazuli and coral, inlaid with floral motifs of precious and semi-precious stones were fashioned by 20,000 artisans in 22 years in order to make the emperor's dream a reality.

In the crypt of Taj Mahal lies the jewel-inlaid cenotaph of the queen, and a little to one side—the only asymmetrical feature in the Taj—the richly decorated casket of the emperor.

The Taj Mahal stands serene, perfect in its garden of cypress trees reflecting water channels on the banks of the River *Yamuna*. The Taj takes a different hue at every time of the day. It glows softly pink at dawn; in the powerful light of the midnoon sun it appears to float in the mirage; at dusk it reflects the fiery tints of the setting sun, and in the moonlight, the pearly white marble mausoleum shimmers silver beautifully as an edifice of the man's concentrated outpourings of romance. The Taj, in all its timeless beauty, is still the inspiration of poets and painters, writers and photographers.

It was the last wish of Mumtaz Mahal which prompted Shah Jahan to build the Taj. Shah Jahan was married to Mumtaz-uz Zamani. He gave the title of 'Mumtaz Mahal' to her at the age of 20. While giving birth to her last child Mumtaz Mahal died. She had expressed three wishes to the emperor. These were; not to marry again, to take care of the children and to raise a tomb over her grave which would not have any parallel in the world.

The Great Fort of Agra

The Agra Fort, built during the reigns of three Mughal emperors, viz. Akbar, Jahangir and Shah Jahan is a fitting monument to the creative and artistic genius of the times. Girdled by massive double walls and pierced by four towering gate ways, the fort is a complex of palaces, courts, mosques, baths, gardens and pleasure pavilions.

The red sandstone Jahangiri Mahal built by Akbar for his Hindu queen, Jodhabai, the mother of Jahangir; the Great Public and Private Audience Halls, the Khas Mahal, the Palace of Mirrors, the Jewel-like Nagina Masjid, the pure white Pearl Mosque built by Shah Jahan; the Garden of Grapes and the Fish Pavilion or Water Garden are the main attractions.

Fatehpur Sikri

Sikri was a village around 40 kilometres away from Agra, and there lived a renowed Sufi mystic, Sheikh Salim Chishti, with supernatural powers. Emperor Akbar came here to seek the blessing of the saint for a son and his prayer was answered.

Thus was born Jahangir who, as a prince was named "Salim" in honour of the saint. As per the advice of Sheikh Salim Chishti to live in Sikri, the emperor found the new city containing the palace complex. After the conquest of Gujarat, Akbar named the village "Fatehpur" (the town of victory) which later came to be known as "Fatehpur Sikri". After 16 short, but, memorable years of living here Akbar returned to Agra.

Even today, the inner citadel is immaculately preserved. The palaces, baths, royal mint, courts and gardens still stand in splended homage to a great visionary and builder. The heart of the palace complex however, is very much alive. For, at the tomb of Sheikh Salim Chishti, a white marble canopy set in the great courtyard of the Royal Mosque, pilgrims still come in thousands to offer flowers, tie a thread in the latticed screens, and to pray for the gift of a son.

The Tomb of Itemad-ud-Daula

It stands in the centre of a Persian garden, an architectural jewel, elegantly designed and exquistely finished. Noorjahan, the brilliant queen of Jahangir, built it for her parents. A precursor of the Taj, this small garden tomb reflects the taste and sophistication of the gifted queen. The warm yellow marble is highlighted with white and black marble inlay, and the lacey pierced marble screens and rich, jewel-inlaid mosaics have a delicate feminine quality that is pure enchantment.

Akbar's Tomb, Sikandara

Sikandara is the final resting place of Emperor Akbar. The emperor began to build his own mausoleum during his life time; a red sandstone monument designed with bold mosaic patterns, in a spacious square garden. A magnificent marble-inlaid gateway leads up to the open airy four-tiered structure which is topped by a white marble cenotaph and screen on the fifth storey. This was added by Jahangir who completed the mausoleum after his father's death.

Accommodation

- Mughal Sheraton, Fatehabad Road, Tajganj.
- Mumtaz, Fatehabad Road, Cantt.
- Agra Deluxe, Fatehabad Road.
- Amar, Fatehabad Road.
- Grand Hotel, 137 Station Road, Cantt.

Ajmer

The city, 146 kilometres from Jaipur, is situated in a basin at the foot of Taragarh Hill and is surrounded by a stone wall with five gateways. It is said that seven pilgrimages to Ajmer equal one to Mecca. Every year, especially at the annual Islamic festivals of Id and Mohurram, thousands of pilgrims converge of this ancient town on the banks of the Ana Sagar Lake in Rajasthan. Ajmer is renowned throughout the Muslim world as the burial place of Mu'inuddin Chishti who claimed descent from the son-in-law of Mohammad. Born in Afghanistan in the middle of the 12th Century, when Islam was on the verge of spreading to India, he visited Ajmer in 1192. He died here in 1235 and his tomb became a place of pilgrimage. Mosques, pavilions and other tombs were subsequently erected.

From Station Road, a walk through the bazaars either to the Dargah/Masjid area or to Akbar's Palace/ Nasiyan Temple area can be very interesting. You can cover both areas in a day.

The **Dargah of Khwaja Mu'inuddin Chishti** is the tomb of the Sufi saint which was begun by Iltutmish and completed by Humayun. Set in the heart of the old town, the entrance is through the bazaar. The Emperor Akbar first made a pilgrimage to the shrine to give thanks for conquering Chittor in 1567, and the second for the birth of his son Prince Salim. From 1570 to 1580 Akbar made almost annual pilgrimages to Ajmer on foot from Agra, and the kos minars along the road from Agra are witness of the popularity of the pilgrimage route. It is considered the second holiest site after Mecca. On their first visit, rich Muslims pay for a feast of rice, ghee, sugar, almonds, raisins and spices to be cooked in one of the large pots in the courtyard inside the high gateway. These are still in regular use. On the right is the Akbar Masjid; to the left, an assembly hall for the poor.

In the inner courtyard is the white marble **Shah Jahan Masjid,** 33m long with 11 arches and a carved balustrade on three sides. In the inner court is the Dargah, also white marble, square with a domed roof and two entrances. The ceiling is gold-embossed velvet, and silver rails and gates enclose the tomb.

Nearby is the **Mazar of Bibi Hafiz Hamal,** daughter of the saint, a small enclosure with marble lattice work. Close by is that of Chimni Begum, daughter of Shah Jahan. She never married, refusing to leave her father during the 7 years he was held captive by Aurangzeb. She spent her last days in Ajmer, as did another daughter who probably died of tuberculosis. At the south end of the Dargah is the Jhalra (tank).

The **Arhai-din-ka Jhonpra Mosque** lies beyond the Dargah in a narrow valley. Originally a Jain college built in 1153, it was partially destroyed by Muhammad of Ghori in 1192, and in 1210 turned into a mosque by Qutb-ud-din-Aibak, who built a massive screen of seven arches in front of the pillared halls, allegedly in 2½ days. The temple pillars which were incorporated in the building are all different. The mosque measures 79m x 17m with 10 domes supported by 124 colums and incorporates older Hindu and Jain masonry. Much of it is in ruins though restoration work was undertaken at the turn of the century; only part of the 67m screen and the Jain prayer hall remain.

Akbar's Palace is in the city centre near the eastern wall. It is a large rectangular building with a fine gate. Today it houses the Government museum.

The ornate **Nasiyan Jain Temple** on Prithviraj Marg has a remarkable museum alongside the Jain shrine, which itself is open only to Jains. Ajmer has a large Jain population, and the Shri Siddhkut Chaiyalaya was founded in 1864 in honour of the first Jain Tirthankar, Rishabdev, by a Jain diamond merchant, Raj Bahadur Seth Moolchand Nemichand Soni. The opening was celebrated in 1895. Behind a wholly unimposing exterior, on its first floor the Svarna Nagari Hall houses an astonishing reconstruction of the Jain conception of the Universe, with gold plated replicas of every Jain shrine in India. Over 1,000kg of gold is estimated to have been used, and at one end of the gallery diamonds have also been placed behind decorative coloured glass, the whole can be seen from different external galleries. The holy mountain, Sumeru, is at the centre of the continent, and around it are such holy sites as Ayodhya, the birth place of the Tirthankar, recreated in gold plate, and a remarkable collection of model temples. On the ground floor, beneath the model, are the various items taken on procession around the town on the Jain festival day of 23rd November each year. The Trustees of the temple are continuing to maintain and embellish it. The Trustees of the temple are continuing to maintain and embellish it. The walls and ceilings of the main hall have been completely re-painted in traditional style since the late 1980s.

Mayo College, 4 km from centre, was founded to provide young Indian princes with a liberal education, one of two genuinely Indo-Saracenic buildings designed by De Fabeck in Ajmer, the other being the Mayo hospital. The College was known as the 'Eton' of Rajputana and was run along the lines of an English Public School. It is now open to all.

Ana Sagar, an artificial lake was further enhanced by Emperors Jahangir and Shah Jahan who added their baradari and pavilions. The Foy Sagar, 5 km, another artificial lake was a famine relief project.

Taragarh, (Star Fort), built by Ajaipal Chauhan in 1100 stands on the hilltop overlooking the town. It is rectangular with walls 4.5 m thick. Along the way is a graveyard of muslim 'Martyrs' who died storming the fort.

Govt. Museum in Akbar's Palace, built in 1570 and restored in 1905. Fine sculpture from 6th to 17th centuries, paintings; old Rajput and Mughal armour and coins, are on view.

Accommodation

- Ajaymeru, Ana Sagar Circular Road.
- Prithviraj, Jaipur Road.
- Regency, Delhi Gate
- Aaram, off Ana Sagar Circular Road, LIC Colony.
- Khadim Hotel, Savitri Girls College Road, Near Bus Station.

Allahabad

On the edge of the pleasant Chander Shekhar Azad Park, in the Civil Lines the grounds of the Allahabad Museum are dotted with pieces of ancient sculpture. Inside, early terracotta artefacts, 8th Century sculptures from the Buddhist site of Kaushambi, and a striking 12th Century image from Khajuraho of Shiva and Parvati. A copious collection of modern Indian art includes work by Haldar, Sajit Khastgir and Rathin Mitra, as well as Jamini Roy, who was inspired by folk art. European paintings concentrate on spiritual themes, with sombre but naïve canvasses by the Russian artist, Nicholas Roerich, and further pieces by the Tibetologist, Lama Angarika Govinda. A natural history section features stuffed animals and birds, and photographs and documents cover the Independence struggle.

North of the museum rise the 19th Century sandstone buildings of Allahabad University, and the Gothic Muir College, built in 1870. A 61 metre-high tower accompanies domes clad with blue and white glazed tiles (some of which are missing), and a quadrangle with tall and elegant arches. Just beyond the college, in beautiful grounds, roughly 1 km northeast of the museum, is Anand Bhavan. This ornate Victorian building, with Indo-Saracenic effects finished in grey and white trim and crowned by a chattri, was the boyhood home of the first Prime Minister of an independent India, Jawaharlal Nehru. It is now maintained as a museum.

Not far from Anand Bhavan, down a small road next to a children's park, is the Bharadwaj Ashram which is not an ashram as such but a collection of small temples. None is particularly old, but the ashram is named after the philosopher, scientist and ascetic Bharadwaj, said in the Ramayana to have had his hermitage here, and to have been visited by Rama. Legend relates that the ashram once had ten thousand students. Unusually, women are numbered among its purohits (priests), and act as caretakers.

A short way south of the main railway station, a lofty gateway leads to the attractive walled gardens of Khusrau Bagh, where the remains of Jahangir's tragic son Khusrau rest in a simple sandstone mausoleum completed in 1622. Khusrau made an unsuccessful bid for power that ended in death at the hands of his brother, Shah Jahan, and is buried far from the centre of Moghul power. His mother's two-storeyed mausoleum is a short way west, beyond a tomb reputed to be that of his sister.

Most of Allahbad's river frontage is along the

Yamuna, to the south where women perform arati or evening worship at Saraswati Ghat by floating diya, small oil-filled lamps, downstream. Immediately to the west, in Minto Park, a memorial marks the exact spot where the British Raj came into being, when India was taken away from the East India Company in 1858 and placed under the auspices of the crown.

Accommodation

- Allahabad Regency, 16 Tashkent Marg
- Milan, 46 Leader Road
- N.C. Continental, Katju Road
- N Cee, Leader Road

Almora

Almora, 67 km north of Nainital, is one of the rare Kumauni towns that conspicuously pre-dates the Raj, with its cobbled alleyways and wood and stone buildings. Founded by the Chand dynasty in 1560, and occupied successively by the Gurkhas and the British, it remains a major market town, and is considered the cultural capital of the region. Set at a pleasant altitude of 1646m rambling ridges that look towards the inner Himalayan snows, Almora's peaceful environs have attracted an electic assortment of visitors over the years, such as Swami Vivekananda, Timothy Leary and the Tibetologist and author of "The way of the white Clouds", Lama Angarika Govinda.

Although most of Almora's official business is conducted along the Mall, the market area immediately above and parallel to it along the crest of the saddle, holds much more of interest. Exploring its well-stocked bazaars, knitted together with lanes, flanked by beautifully carved wooden facades, you feel as though you're drifting into the distant past. The great local tradition is the manufacture of tamta, beaten copper pots plated with silver, which are sold in the busy Lala Bazaar and the Chowk area at the northeast end of the market.

Towards the top of town, beyond Chowk, a compound holds a group of Chand period stone temples. The main one, a squat single-storey structure, is dedicated to Nanda Devi, the goddess embodied in the region's highest mountain. More typical or Kumauni Temple architecture are two larger Shaivite painted stone temples, capped with umbrella-like wooden roofs covering their stone amalaka (circular crowns). During Sravana (Jul/Aug) a large fair is held here in honour of Nanda Devi.

Enclosures amid the tall pine woods of Deer Park, a pleasant three-kilometre walk northeast of the Mall, house assorted deer, as well as Himalayan black bear and sorry looking leopards. Following the Mall southwest for three kilometres, on the other hand, brings you to the hill called Bright End Corner where you may, weather permitting, catch view of the hills and vales of Kumaun, and the distant snow peaks.

Accommodation

- Kailas
- KMVN Tourist Bungalow
- Renuka
- Savoy, Police Line
- Shikhar

Ambala

Ambala, 202 kilometres from Delhi became a large British cantonment, laid out from 1843 onwards in grid fashion. The famous Gupta iron pillar now at the Qutab Minar in Delhi was originally on the hill just outside Ambala town before being moved by the Muslim rulers to its present position. Paget Park on the northern side of the city is a pleasant open space with the shell of St. John's Cathedral, designed in 14th Century Gothic Style. It was bombed in the 1965 Indo-Pakistan war. The city is the headquaters of the district and an important wheat market. Today it is also well-known as an important centre of small-scale industry, notably the manufacture of scientific instruments.

Accommodation

- Four Seasons
- Kingfisher (Haryana Tourisum)

Amritsar

Amritsar is about 500 kilometres from Delhi and nearly 260 kilometres from Ambala. The Golden Temple also known as, *Harminder Sahib* in Amritsar, the city which is a pool of nectar; is considered the holiest shrine of the sikh community, and is more than 400 years old. Roofed over with gilded copper, this astonishingly beautiful marble temple built next to an enclosed pool, which is considered sacred, is a holy site venerated by Hindus and Sikhs alike. Its domes were covered in gold leaf in the early 19th century by the Sikh ruler, Maharana Ranjit Singh.

Accommodation

- Mohan International, Albert Road.
- Airlines, Cooper Road.
- Astoria, 1, Queens Road.
- Palace, Station Links Road.

Anandpur Sahib

The town 'The City of divine bliss', Anandpur Sahib, 340 kilometres from Delhi, was established by the 9th Guru, Tegh Bahadur, in 1664, when the Sikhs had been forced into the foothills of the Himalayas by increasing Mughal opposition. It is in a picturesque setting at the foot of the Shiwaliks on the east bank of the River Sutlej. Guru Tegh Bahadur was executed at Chandni Chowk in Delhi, and his severed head was brought to Anandpur Sahib to be cremated. This event contributed to the determination of the 10th Guru, Gobind Singh, Tegh Bahadur's Son, to forge a new body to protect the Sikh Community. The Khalsa Panth was thus created on Baisakhi Day in 1699. Anandpur Sahib became both a fortress and a school of Sikh learning. Hola Mohalla is celebrated the day after Holi when battles are re-enacted using old weapons. There is a small museum dedicated to the memory of Guru Tegh Bahadur recounting the history of the Sikhs in a series of paintings.

Accommodation

- Champa Tourist Huts

Anantnag

Anantnag on the wáy to Srinagar, about 180 kilometres from Jammu, has a series of springs. Close to it is Mattan (ancient name Martand) with a holy spring over which a temple of the Sun God has been built. Anantnag is known for its wood turning and gabba making crafts. In recent years, crewel embroidery and carpet weaving have become specialities here.

Badrinath

In the Himalayan range, there are many holy places and ancient temples, connected with the Hindu mythology. The peace and solemnity prevalent, and the mountain range atmosphere is very suitable for a religious pilgrimage and yogic meditation. The places of interest from the point of view of scenic beauty, peace and tranquility besides of considerable importance to Hindu pilgrims are Badrinath, Kedarnath, Gangotri and Yamunotri, each of which can be reached from Rishikesh, about 230 kilometres from Delhi.

Temple of Sri Badrinathji

The legend has it that River Ganga was requested to descend to earth from the hairlocks of Lord Shiva, for saving human beings from drought. As it was felt that if Ganga descended on the earth at one place, the earth would not have been able to withstand the force of her descent, the mighty Ganga split into 12 channels and descended at different places. Alaknanda where the temple of Sri Badrinath is located is one of such holy places, about 510 kilometres away from Delhi and 280 kilometres from Rishikesh through mountain tracks. A vehicle can go right upto the temple precints.

The legend dates the temple back to the Vedic age. The present temple is believed to have been established by Adi Sankaracharya, the 8th Century A.D. Hindu saint and reformist who also established a math here.

Takta Kund, Surya Kund, and **Narad Kund** are natural thermal springs on the bank of Alaknanda.

Mata Murti Temple is devoted to mother of Sri Badrinathji.

Vyas Gufa, Ganesh Gufa, Bhimpul and **Vasundhara Falls.** All these places, located near Badrinath, figure prominently in Hindu mythology.

Accommodation

- Devlok

Bharatpur Bird Sanctuary

About 176 kilometres from Delhi, 55 kilometres from Agra and nearly 27 kilometres from Fatehpur Sikri, is situated, in Bharatpur within the confines of an early 18th Century Rajput fort, Keoladeo Ghana, one of the finest water bird sanctuaries in the world.

The 40 kilometere area of the sanctuary has 1,100 hectares of marsh habitat surrounded by a fine scrub forest, with the largest concentration and variety of bird-life in Asia.

Motorable embankments divide the sanctuary into compartments. Trees growing on these, sub-merged in the water, provide excellent perching roosting and heronry sites for the water birds. Over 120 bird species are resident in this area and breed here regularly. The sanctuary hosts hundreds of migrant species each winter and nearly 350 species of resident and migratory birds have been recorded here. Keoladeo is the only surviving wintering ground in India of the endangered Siberian cranes. A gradually diminishing number of these birds has been arriving each successive winter, from their breeding grounds 6400 kilometres away in

Siberia.

The bird diversity of Keoladeo includes various species of storks, cranes, ibises, cormorants, ducks and geese, waders, plovers, king-fishers, rollers, bee-eaters, raptors, scavengers, owls, song-birds, pelicans, herons pigeons and doves, partridges and a profusion of grassland and scrub birds. The surrounding forest has wild boar, chitam, sambhar, nilgai, black buck, mongoose, otter, python, monitor, lizard, jungle cat, fishing cat, jackal, fox, porcupine and hare. The marshes abound in fish life, water snakes, turtles and amphibians.

Accommodation

- Bharatpur Forest Lodge
- Saras, Fatehpur Sikri Road
- Shanti Kutir Rest House, Near Noating Jetly
- Bambino, Near Park Entrance

Bikaner

Bikaner is 538 kilometres away from Delhi.

It is definitely worth spending a day or two simply wandering around Bikaner, watching dyers at work, visiting the ancient Jain temples, and discovering the delights of Junagarh Fort. Bikaner is also famous for its skilled lacquer work and attractive handicrafts, and the markets are full of good buys.

Junagarh Fort

Built on ground level, defended only by high walls and a wide moat, Junagarh Fort is not as immediately imposing as the mighty hill forts elsewhere in Rajasthan. But the decorative interiors and sculpted stone of the palaces, temples and thirty-seven pavilions within its walls are almost unrivalled in their magnificence.

The fort was constructed between 1587 and 1593, during the rule of Rai Singh, and later rulers added their own palatial suites, temples and plush courtyards. The Karan Mahal, with gold-leaf paintings adorning its pillars and walls, was built in the 17th Century to commemorate a victory over the Mughal emperor,

Aurangazeb, while the imaginatively painted Chandra Mahal and the dazzling Phool Mahal were erected by Gaj Singh, a hundred years later.

Stained-glass windows, finely carved stone and wood balconies, and brightly painted walls and ceilings throughout the fort leave no doubt as to the extravagant tastes of these rulers, or the skills of the artisans they employed. The Anup Mahal is perhaps the most opulent, with wooden ceilings inlaid with mirrors, Italian tiles and delicate lattice work on the windows and balconies. The most recent part of the fort, dating from 1937, it houses part of the museum, whose exhibits include the inevitable weaponry and an unexpected World War II aeroplane, still in tip-top condition.

The Old City

Kote Gate at the west end of MG Road is the main entrance through the high city walls into the atmospheric old city, where the clashing and banging of metalworkers resonate through the winding streets tinted with the hues of local dyers. The main attractions here are the two Jain temples in the southwest corner. Built by two merchant brothers, both are remarkable for the sheer mass of colour and intricate designs of wall paintings, a rare feature in Rajasthan's Jain temples.

The ground floor of Bhandreshwar temple has a cluster of pillars; some are decorated with gilded floral design known as *usta* typical of Muslim artisans, others with embossed male and female sulptures common in medieval India. A statue of Lord Suminath, the fifth *tirthankara,* stands on the second floor. Sandeshwar temple, dedicated to Neminath and dated to 1536, houses rows of saints shaped from solid marble, and has enamel and gold-leaf paintings on the walls.

The 16th Century, Laxminath temple nearby was built by Lunkaran Singh, the third ruler of Bikaner, on the edge of the high city wall. It overlooks a Muslim Community of dyers and screen printers with the barren desert in the distance.

Lalgarh Palace

The sturdy red-sandstone Lalgarh Palace in the north of town is home to the royal family of Bikaner, although parts now serve as a hotel. It was built during the reign of Ganga Singh, who lived there from 1902, using the fort only for private business. Despite some detailed carving, its modern aspect makes it fairly dull in comparison to other Rajasthani palaces.

Ganga Golden Jubilee Museum

The small Ganga Golden Jubilee Museum on NH8 near the Tourist Bungalow contains a moderately interesting display of costumes, weapons, ornaments, ancient statues and paintings, one of which depicts the signing of the Versailles Treaty by Ganga Singh. Older exhibits include terracottas belonging to the Gupta period.

Accommodation

- Amit, Station Road
- Delux, Station Road
- RTDC Dhola Maru Tourist Bungalow
- Green, Station Road
- Joshi, Station Road

Chamba

Chamba, in Haryana, is 585 kilometres away from Delhi. Shielded on all sides by high mountains, and protected by forces in Kangra to the south, Chamba was ruled for over a millennium by kings descended from Raja Singh Varma, who founded it in 920 AD.

In summer, Gujjars, normadic Muslim dairymen, wheel great urns of milk through the streets, and migratory Gaddi shepherds gather in Chamba before moving south to Kangra. The *Chowgan,* a large green used for sports, evening strolls and festive celebrations marks the centre of town, over-looked by the Rang Mahal Palace, now a college.

Lakshmi Narayan Temples

The intimate complex of Lakshmi Narayan temples, behind Dogra Bazaar west of the *Chowgan,* is of a style found only in Chamba and Brahmour. Three of its six earth-brown temples are dedicated to Vishnu and three to Shiva, all with profusely carved outer walls and curious curved shikharas, topped with overhanging wooden canopies and gold pinnacles added in 1678 in definance of Aurangzeb's order to destroy all Hindu temples in the hill states.

Entering the compound, you are confronted by the largest and oldest temple, built in the 10th Century. It enshrines an idol of Lakshmi Narayan (Vishnu), sculpted in Rajasthani marble. Female deities flanking the entrance to the sanctuary, each holding a water vessel, represent the rivers Ganga and Yamuna, while the interior is decorated with scenes from the Mahabharata and Ramayana. One shows Vishnu with a lotus stem emerging form his navel that blooms with six flowers, each supporting a separate god. Temples dedicated to Shiva, watched over by a ferocious statue of half-man half-bird Garuda, the destroyer of obstacles who also serves as Vishnu's mount, fill the third courtyard. Among the images on the outer walls, shiva's consort is depicted in her various forms as Parvati, Durga, Gauri and Uma. In the inner sanctuary, once your eyes are accustomed to the dim light, you'll see sturdy brass images of Shiva, Parvati and Nandi, inlaid with silver and copper brought from mines nearby.

Bhuri Singh Museum

This museum, opposite Sham Singh hospital at the south end of the *Chowgan,* bolds a reasonable display of arts and crafts. It has several 18th and 19th Century Kangra miniature paintings. Other stems on display are statues, sculptures, silver jewellery, heavy bronzes from Chamba, early coins, murals, and *rumals* like embroidered paintings, depicting scenes from popular myths.

Accommodation

- Hotel Chamunda
- HPTDC Hotel Iravati
- Rishi, opp. Lakshmi Narayan Temples.

Chittaurgarh (Chittor)

This is one of the oldest cities in Rajasthan, founded in 728 by Bappu Rawak, who according to legend was reared by the Bhil tribe. Chittaurgarh is located at 116 kilometres from Udaipur and 167 kilometres from Ajmer.

Two sites near the river Berach have shown stone tools dating from the Lower Palaeolithic; Buddhist relics from a few centuries BC. From the 7th Century it was occupied by succession of rulers. Invading Muslim armies saw the strategic importance of the imposing fort sited on a rocky outcrop of the Aravallis, and from the 12th Century when it became the centre of Mewar.

Excavations in the Mahasati area of the fort have shown four shrines with ashes and charred bones, the earliest dating from about the 11th century AD. There was a paved platform over which was a sati stone, commemorating the self immolating of a widow, and two other loose sati stones were also discovered.

The fort dominates the city and is itself 280 ha in area. Until 1568 the town was situated within the walls. Today the lower town sprawls to the west of the fort and straddles the Berach and Gambheri rivers.

The fort stands on a 152 m high rocky hill rising abruptly above the surrounding plain. The great length of the walls (5 km), however, makes the elevation look lower than it really is. The ruins are deserted and the slopes are covered with scrub jungle. The modern town lies at the foot of the hill and is surrounded by a wall. Access is across a limestone bridge of 10 arches over the Gambheri River. The winding 1.5 km ascent to the fort is defended by seven impressive gates: the Padal Pol, is where rawat Bagh Singh, the Rajput leader, fell during the second siege; the Bhairon or Tuta (broken) Pol, where Jaimal, one of the heroes of the third siege was killed by Akbar in 1567 (chhattris to Jaimal and patta); The Hanuman Pol and Ganesh Pol; the Jola (joined) Gate whose upper arch is connected to the Lakshman Pol; finally the Ram Pol (1459) which is the main gate. Inside the walls is a village and ruined palaces, towers and temples.

Rana Kumbha's Palace

On the right immediately inside the fort are the ruins of the palace (1433-68), originally built of dressed stone with a stucco covering. It is approached by two gateways, the large, Badi Pol and the three-bay deep, Tripolia. Once there were elephant and horse stables, the zenanas (recognised by the jali screen), and a Sina temple. The jauhar committed by Padmini and her followers is believed to have taken place beneath the courtyard. The north frontage of the palace contains an attractive combination of canopied balconies. Across from the palace is the archaeological office and the Nau Lakha Bhandar (The Treasury, **nau lakha**-900,000). The temple to Rana Kumbha's wife Mira Bai who was a renowned poetess is visible from the palace and stands close to the Kumbha Shyama Temple. The older 11th century Jain Sat Bis Deori Temple with its 27 shrines, is nearby. The Shringara Chauri Temple, (1456) near the fort entrance, has sculptured panels of musicians, warriors and Jain deities.

Rana Ratan Singh's Palace is to north by the Ratneshwar Lake. Built in stone around 1530 it too had stucco covering. Originally rectangular in plan and enclosed within a high wall, it was subsequenly much altered. The main gate to the south still stands as an example of the style employed.

To the east of Rana Kumbha's Palace is the early 20th Century Fateh Prakash Palace built by Maharana Fateh Singh which houses an interesting museum containing archaeological finds from this site. To the south is the Vijay Stambha 1458-68, one of the most interesting buildings in the fort, built by Rana Kumbha to celebrate his victory over Mahmud Khilji of Malwa in 1440. Visible for miles around, it stands on a base 14m square and 3m high, and rises 37m. The 9-storeyed sandstone tower, which has been restored was covered with sculpture from the Hindu pantheon; the upper section retains some of the original. Nearby is the Mahasati terrace where the ranas were cremated when Chittaurgarh was the capital of Mewar. There are also numerous sati stones. Just to the south is the Samadhishvara Temple to Siva, dating from 11th and 15th Centuries with some good sculptured friezes. Steps down lead to the deep Gomukh Kund, where the sacred spring water enters through a stone carved as a cow's mouth.

Proceding along the path to the south, the Palaces of Jaimal and Patta, renowned for their actions during the siege of 1567, stand side by side. The former's austere facde has a single opening for a door, the horizontal lines mark out three storys where, in reality, there are only two! Patta's Palace was based on the zenana building of Rana Kumbha's Palace, and is more interesting. You then pass the Bhimtal before seeing the Kalika Mata Temple with exterior carvings and the ruins of Chonda's House with its three storey domed tower. Chonda did not claim the title when his father, Rana Lakha, died in 1421.

Padmini's Palace further south, originally late 13 Century, was rebuilt at the end of the 19th. The small pleasure palace sited in the middle of the lake has pretty gardens around it. Ala-ud-din Khilji is said to have seen Padmini's beautiful reflection in the water through a mirror on the palace wall. This striking vision convinced him that she had to be his.

You pass the deer park on your way round to the Suraj Pol (Sun Gate) and pass the Adbhutanatha Temple to Siva before reaching the second tower, the Kirti Stambh, a Tower of Fame. Fergus on has described it as one of the most interesting Jain monuments of the age. Smaller than the Vijay Stambha with only seven storeys, it is dedicated to Adinath, the first Jain Tirthankara. Naked figures of Tirthankaras are repeated several hundred times on the face of the tower. A Narrow internal staircase goes to the top.

Of particular interest are the number of tanks and wells in the fort that have survived the centuries. Water, from both natural and artificial sources, was harnessed to provide an uniterrupted supply to the people. The good management of water was achieved by keeping animals away from the source of drinking water.

Accommodation

- Castle Bijaipur
- Padmini, Chanderiya Road
- Panna Tourist Bungalow
- Janta Avas Grih, Station Road
- Natraj, Near Bus Stand

Chandigarh

Chandigarh located at a distance of 247 kilometres from Delhi is made up of 47 numbered sectors, subdivided into lettered blocks. Le Corbusier conceived of the city plan as a living organism, with the imposing Capital Complex to the north as a "head", the shopping precinct, Sector 17, a "heart", the green open spaces as "lungs", and the cross-cutting network of roads, separated into eight different grades for use by various types of vehicles a "circulatory system". A rickshaw can get around the few noteworthy sights in two to three hours.

The Museum and Gallery

Chandigarh's large museum and art gallery, five minutes by rickshaw north of the city centre in Sector 10, houses a sizeable and informatively displayed collection of ancient sculpture, miniature paintings and contemporary Indian art. Among prize pieces on the first floor are a dozen or so standing Buddhas from Gandhara, noted for their delicately carved "Wet-look" lunghis and distinctly Hellenic features— a legacy of Alexander the Great's conquests. Also Greek-influenced are the beautiful terracotta heads mounted in glass cases at the top of the main staircase; they date from the 1st and 2nd Centuries BC.

Art enthusiasts will find plenty to pore over in the adjacent gallery, where abundant exquisite Moghul, Kangra, and Rajasthani miniatures are accompanied by interpretive panels outlining the main features of the respective schools. Modern works featured in the last room include a couple of AN Tagore's atmospheric watercolours, five original Roerichs, and several over-the-top patriotic and devotional Sikh canvasses.

The Capital Complex

Three blocks north of downtown, in the stadow of Shivalik Hills, the capital complex, sector 1, is the site of some of Le Corbusier's most ambitious experiments.

The most imposing edifice in the group is the eight-storey Secretariat, Chandigarh's highest building which houses Haryana and Panjab's ministerial offices, and has a roof garden with good views over the city. The resemblance of the Legislature Assembly, or Vidhan Sabha, just north to a power station is no coincidence: Le Corbusier was allegedly inspired by a stack of cooling towers he saw in Ahmedabad. The most colourful of the three buildings stands opposite the Secretariat. Said to incorporate elements of the Buland Darwaza in Fatehpur Sikri, the High Court, whose double roof symbolizes the protective power of the law, is decorated inside with huge woollen tapestries.

The Rock Garden

Close to the Capital Complex, and a refreshing counterpoint to Le Corbusier's drab concrete cityscape, is the bizarre Rock Garden — a surreal fantasyland fashioned from fragments of shattered plates, neon strip lights, pots, pebbles, broken bangles and assorted urban-industrial junk. The open-air exhibition is the lifelong labour of a retired Public Works Department road inspector, Nek Chand. Inspired by a recurrent childhood dream, he spent seven years scouring the stream beds of the Shivalik Hill for materials, and another nine on site before his vision was revealed to the public in 1976.

The Rock Garden has expanded into a labyrinthine four-acre site that comprises more than a dozen different enclosures, interconnected by narrow passages, arched walkways, streams, and tiny bridges. Teeming on weekends with excited children and their parents, the complex also features several sculptural set-pieces: mostly birds, animals, and human figures, whose rigid stance and transfixed facial expressions take their cue from Indian adivasi art.

Accommodation

- Alankar, sector 22 A
- Amar, 806-6 Udyog Path, Sector 22 A
- Aroma, Himalaya Marg, Sector 22C
- Baliji Tourist Bungalow, 534 Sector 36B
- Chandigarh Tourist Bungalow, 97 Sector 21-A

Corbett National Park

Three hundred kilometres from Delhi is Corbett's National Park, a place worthwhile visiting, with picturesque landscape with blue waters, the rounded boulders of the Ram Ganga and the backdrop of the well covered Himalayas. The Sal forests present a three-dimensional effect in the forests.

The 520 sq. km. wildlife sanctuary is abundant in its population of tiger, elephant, leopard, black bear, deer, python and river animals. The reserve supports over 100 tigers with the highest density of the tiger population in the country, of a tiger to every 5 kilometres. Over 585 species of birds also thrive here.

Accommodation

- Tiger Tops Corbett Lodge
- Corbett JungleResort
- Corbett Ramganga Resort
- Corbett Riverside Resort

Dalhousie

Dalhousie owes its name to Lord Dalhousie, Governer General of Punjab, attracted by the cool climate to establish a sanitorium here for the many British, who, like himself, suffered ill health. Dalhousie is most usually approached by bus from Pathankot in Punjab, 80km southwest. The steep path that climbs the hill from the bus stand towards the Mall is the shortest route to the centre.

From the central Gandhi Chowk, narrow roads lead west to the bus stand and south to another crossroad, Subhash Chowk, as well as dropping southwest to the army cantonment. The Mall, in the north of town affords splendid views to high snow-capped peaks. Forest tracks snake around the hillsides, linking the main roads. The one between Gandhi and Subhash chowks dips beneath overhanging pines, and passes rocks painted in bold bright colours with the Buddhist goddesss Tara and Tibetan prayers. Further south, a thin road leads to Panch Pulla, where five bridges span a rushing stream and a memorial commemorates the freedom fighter Ajit Singh, a firm supporter of the left-wing Congressman Subash Chandra Bose who raised the Indian National Army to fight alongside the Japanese during World War II. The road north out of Gandhi Chowk meanders up the hill to Bakrota, where a small community of weavers make traditional Tibetan carpets.

Accommodation

- Aroma & Claire's, Court Road.
- Chaanakya, The Mall.
- Grand View, Bus Stand.
- Moonlight, Panch Pulla Road.

Delhi

Delhi, the capital of India, is one of the fastest growing cities. Delhi is the only city which has something of everything which one can see in India; people of all races, religions, languages. It has ancient temples, mosques, mausolea, palaces, castles, congested markets, bustling commercial complexes, skycrapers, residential colonies, parks, spacious gardens, wide open vistas lined by flowering trees and a baffling variety of flora and fauna.

Delhi has some of the finest museums in the country. Its boutiques and shopping arcades offer access to a wealth of traditional and contemporary crafts from all over the country.

History of Delhi dates back to the first millennium BC. Excavations revealed that the place was *Indraprastha*, a site associated with the Hindu epic *Mahabharata*. The present Delhi has spread far beyond the confines of the "seven cities" created between the 13th and the 17th centuries, such as *Lal Kot* and *Quila Rai Pithora* created by Rajput Kings, *Siri* created by Allaudin Khilji. *Tughlaqabad*, *Jahanpanah*, *Firoz*

Shah Kotla and *Purana Qila* built by Humayun and Sher Shah Suri and *Shahjahanabad* founded by the Mughal emperor Shah Jahan.

The British empire had struck its roots in Calcutta. The new imperial city—New Delhi—was designed by Sir Edward Lutyens for shifting the capital from Calcutta in 1911. Compared to old Delhi, which is congested, with narrow lanes, New Delhi is well planned with spacious avenues, parks, wide roads etc.

Red Fort (Lal Qila)

The Red Fort was the 17th Century imperial citadel ordered by Shah Jahan, one of the Mughal emperors and is mainly made of sandstone. The marble palaces are ornamented with exquisite *pietra dura.*

When Shah Jahan decided to shift the Mughal Empire's capital to Delhi, he built *Shahjahababad*, which is presently known as the walled city of old Delhi. He first enclosed the city by high battlements and bastions with eight gates for entrance and exit. The Red Fort was built thereafter along the banks of the *Jamuna* river. Within the fort, Shah Jahan built a hall for public audience known as *Diwani-i-Aam*, and another one for private audience, *Diwan-e-Khas*, besides apartments and harems. A garden *Hayat Baksh* (life-giving) was also laid out, criss-crossed with canals and fountains. On formal occasions, the Emperor used to sit on the legendary "Peacock Throne", which was inlaid with precious stones.

The Diwan-e-Khas still bears testimony to the splendours of the royal residence with a Persian inscription, the meaning of which in English reads somewhat like this:

"If there be a paradise on Earth,
It is here, it is here, it is here,"

Moti Masjid (Pearl Mosque) in the Red Fort complex was built by Aurangzeb, the son of Shah Jahan.

The Monsoon Pavilions in the complex were built by the last Emperor of the Mughal dynasty, Bahadur Shah who was exiled by the British in 1857.

Jama Masjid

Shah Jahan also built the royal mosque, *Jama Masjid* reckoned by many people as the most beautiful and the largest mosque in the world.

Qutab Minar

Qutb ud din Aibak — a slave of Mohammad of Ghor, after proclaiming himself the Sultan of Delhi and occupying the Rajput Fort built by Hindu Tomar Rajputs, raised a towering minaret, which later came to be known as Qutab Minar. For commemorating his victory, he also built the *Quwwatul Islam Mosque* (the might of Islam) after destroying 27 Hindu and Jain temples with rows and arcades with pillars festooned with beautiful sculptures of Gods and Goddesses, *Apsaras* and Mythical entities, in *Lal Kot*.

The standard of Lord Vishnu, the famous uncorroded and non-rusted Iron Pillar, which is a 2000 years old marvel of the ancient science, still stands in the middle of the courtyard of the Mosque.

A towering symbol of Delhi, the Qutab Minar, ascends a dramatic height of 72.5 metres in five tiers of fluted red and beige sandstone and marble with verses of the *Quran* decorating it.

One of the builders of Qutab Minar lies burried some distance away from the western wall of the *Quwwatul Islam Mosque*.This small tomb has three styles of Arbic calligraphy on its walls.

The Southern entrance to the mosque was the contribution of Sultan Alauddin Khilji. This gate known as "*Alai Darwaza*" is an architectural masterpiece with a high vaulted dome; and the inscriptions from *Quran* in different coloured stones and marble. One can also see a stub of a tower in the complex. This is the *Alai Minar*, named after the Sultan Alauddin Khilji who had planned to build another tower taller than Qutab Minar. The work was left incomplete as Alauddin Khilji died before the tower could make any progress.

Purana Quila

The impressive *Purana Qila* is the result of a combined effort of Humayun, the second emperor of the Mughal dynasty and the Afghan, Sher Shah Suri, who deposed him for a short while. The fort contains a fine mosque and a structure of what was possibly a library.

Jantar Mantar

Located within the modern day New Delhi, on Sansad Marg (near Connaught Circus) is *Jantar Mantar*, an observatory built by Maharaja Jai Singh of Jaipur, in 1724. A giant sun dial reads the time of the day by the falling shadow of the sun on its quadrangles. Another structure in this observatory consists of two circular buildings with a pillar in the centre, where the distance of heavenly bodies can be calculated.

Humanyun's Tomb

Humayun's Tomb is a magnificient one. It is said to be a precursor to the Taj Mahal.

Central Vista

The central vista in New Delhi comprise the Secretariate (North and South Blocks), Viceroy's House (presently the Rashtrapati Bhawan) and circular building of the Parliament. These are superb sandstone landmarks. Sir Edwin Lutyens designed the Rashtrapati Bhawan, whereas the two Secretariate Blocks were designed by Sir Herbert Baker.

India Gate

India Gate at the end of the road from the central vista—Raj Path—is the War Memorial Arch constructed in 1911 to commemorate the soldiers martyred in World War I, designed by Sir Edwin Lutyens.

Tughlaqabad

At Tughlaqabad, one can see the remains of what was once a magnificent city and the capital of Northern India—the city of the Tughlaq dynasty, which ruled this part from 1320 to 1413 — built by Ghiayasuddin Tughlaq. The fort was raised mainly as a protection against Mughal raids. The fort and the tomb are characterestic of Tughlaq architecture.

Bahai Temple

One of the newest monuments of New Delhi is the Lotus Temple built entirely of marble, a house of faith dedicated to the city by the followers of the Bahai religion. The architecture of the lotus shaped temples is stunning and overlooks water pools and landscaped gardens.

Surajkund

Located about 24 kilometres from Delhi, *Suraj Kund* is known for the sun temple built by a Rajput ruler of the Tomar dynasty, around 700 AD.

It is an architectural specimen that had been built by Raja Suraj Pal. It consits of a Romanesque ancient amphitheatre with broad stairs leading down to a pool (*kund*). On its western end are the ruins of a temple with the entrance facing east to catch the rays of the rising sun (*sooraj*).

Accommodation

- Ashok, 50-B Chanakyapuri
- Holiday Inn Crown Plaza, Barakhamba Raod
- Le Meridien, Windsor Place
- Connaught Palace
- Marina, Connaught Circus
- Janpath Hotel, Janpath
- Kanishka, 19 Ashok Road
- Broadway, 4/15A, Asaf Ali Road

Dehradun

Dehradun is about 200 kilometers from Delhi.

Dehradun was developed by the British as a centre of education and research. Among the most important are the Forest Research Institute (1914) set in fine lawns and forests surrounding the impressive red-brick building; the Royal Indian Military Academy (1932), which opened with 40 cadets, but which now takes 1,200. Modelled on Sandhurst, all officers in the Indian army undergo their initial training here. The Doon School, India's first public school, is still one of its most prestigious. The Survey of India (founded 1767, whose Surveyor Generals included Sir George Everest) has its headquarters here.

Dehradun is a pleasant place to relax in or stop en route to Mussoorie. The cantonment across the Bindal Rao is spacious and well wooded. The Mussoorie road is lined with very attractive houses. The main shopping areas are Rajpur Road, Paltan Bazar and Astley Hall; selling handwoven woollens, brassware and jewellery. The nearby Tapkesvar Cave Temple is in a pleasant setting at Shahasradhara, 14 km from

Dehradun, where one can bathe in the cool sulphur springs. Robber's Cave (8 km), Lakshman Sidh(12 km), the snows at Chakrata (9 km) are also within easy reach.

Accommodation

- Madhuban, 97 Rajpur Road
- Ajanta Continental, 101 Rajpur Road
- Hilton, 54 Haridwar Road
- Drona, 45 Gandhi Road
- Kwality, 19 Rajpur Road

Dharamshala

Dharamshala is the principal township of the region and magnificantly set to the background of the Dhauladhar mountains. This place, in Himachal Pradesh, is located at about 160 kilometres from Amritsar and 80 kilometres approximately from Pathankot. Pine forests cover the hillsides and numerous streams cut a path through them, allowing exciting opportunities for fishing.

War Memorial

At the entrance, there exists a beautifully designed monument, raised in the memory of those who laid down their lives for their motherland.

St. John's Church

St. John's Church is a memorial dedicated to Lord Edgin, one of the Viceroys of India who died at Dharamshala; and was buried there, in 1863.

Chinmaya Tapovan

This is a serene Ashram Complex, established by a great exponent of Bhagavad Gita, Swami Chinmayananda. This is the right place where one can acquire knowledge about the teachings of Gita.

Jawalamukhi Temple

This is a unique temple, where there is no idol. An eternal flame that issues from a well in the rock sanctum is being considered as the manifestation of the Goddess and being worshipped. The temple is located in a picturesque environment.

Chamunda Devi

Located by the Baner Stream, to the backdrop of the mighty Dhauladhar mountains is the temple dedicated to Goddess Chamunda Devi who, it is believed, has the boon to grant the desires of those who worship her. Behind the temple there is a cave where a natural stone *Lingam* is worshipped as a manifestation of Lord Shiva.

Other temples in the neighbourhood are of Goddess Chintpurni, and of Brajreshwari.

Trekking and Watersports

Dal lake is a picturesque picnic spot, besides providing a good trekking base.

The 20 kilometre stretch of river between Nadaun and Hamirpur, and the Pong Dam reservoir are ideal for fishing and water sports.

Accommodation

- Him Giri, Naddi
- Udechee Huts, Naddi

Dudhwa National Park

Background

Dudhwa is 238 km north of Lucknow and was designated a National Park in 1977. The area was a reserve since 1879 which had been declared a sanctuary in 1965. The terrain and vegetation is that of the terai. Bordering the Sarda River in the Terai, it is very similar to the Corbett National Park. It has *Sal* forest (in addition to *Shesham, Asna, Khair, Sagaun*), tall savannah grasslands and large marshy areas which are watered by the Neora and Sohel rivers.

Wildlife

The swamps covered with thick tall grass are the ideal habitat of the *Barasingha* (swamp deer with 12 tined antlers, *Cervus ducanceh*), best seen in the Sathiana and Kakraha blocks. The tiger population in Dudhwa is believed to be a third of the offical census of 104 (there have been reports of man-eaters). Dudhwa also has sambar, nilgai, some sloth bears (*Melulus ursinus*), fishing cats and a few leopards; the one-horned rhino has been introduced from east India. The

400 species of avifauna includes Bengal floricans, pied and great Indian Hornbills and king vultures. It also attracts a great variety of water birds (Swamp Partridge, eastern White stork) in addition to birds of prey (osprey, hawks, fishing eagles).

Open 15 Nov-15 June. The best season for viewing large game: Mar-Jun.

Accommodation

- Forest Resthouse
- Tharw Huts
- Log Huts

Gangotri

Gangotri is about 480 kilometre from Delhi and 250 kilometres approximately from Rishikesh, through mountain tracks. A vehicle can go right up to the temple precints.

Gangotri is one of the 12 channels which came into being when Ganga split while descending on earth. The source of Ganga-Gangotri glacier "Gomukh" is nearly 19 kilometres further up from the Temple of Ganga.

According to mythology, Raja Bhagirath used to worship Lord Shiva at the sacred stone near which the temple is located, for the purpose of bringing Ganga down to earth.

Gulmarg

Gulmarg's legendary beauty, its prime location and its proximity to Srinagar (only about 50 kilometres) make it one of the premier hill resorts in the country. The journey to Gulmarg is half the enchantment of reaching there—roads bordered by rigid avenues of rice fields interpersed with picturesque villages.

Gulmarg is a flower-strewn meadow, in the shape of a bowl. It's undulating expanse is grassy slopes for most part, and encirled by fir-clad hills and in the distance snow-dusted peaks. The eleven-kilometre circular road around Gulmarg, offers a magnificent view of much of Kashmir Valley because of it's attitude. In winter, the snow covered slopes and inclines of Gulmarg offer excellent opportunities for skiing.

Gulmarg is one of the world's few resorts to offer the ultimate adventure of hills skiing. A helicopter can take the skiers to a peak from where they can choose their own descent routes.

There are a host of other winter sports, such as toboganning, snow hobbing, snow scootering etc., which can be enjoyed in and around Gulmarg.

Accommodation

- Affarwat
- Highlands Park
- Nedous
- New Zum Zum
- New Tourist Bungalow

Haridwar

At Haridwar the gate (dwar) of God (Hari) - 214 km northeast of Delhi, the River Ganges emerges from its final rapids past the Siwalik Hills, to commence the long slow journey across northern India to the Bay of Bengal. Stretching for roughly 3 km along a narrow strip of land between the craggy wooded hills to the west and the river to the east, Haridwar is especially revered by Hindus, for whom its revered Har-Ki-Pairi ghat, literally the "Footstep of God", marks the exact spot where the river leaves the mountains. Looking north along the vast Doon valley, the faint lines of the Himalayan foothills can be discerned rising above Rishikesh in the distance, while Haridwar itself faces east across the river to the hills of the Rajaji National Park. A major road and rail junction, linking Delhi and the Gangetic plains with the mountains of Uttarkhand and their holy yatra network, Haridwar possesses a crucial spiritual and geographical significance.

Along with Nasik, Ujjain, and the holiest of them all, Prayag in Allahabad, Haridwar is one of the four holy *tirthas* that serve as the focus of the massive

Kumbh Mela Festival. Every twelve years, thousands of pilgrims come to bathe at a pre-ordained moment in the turbulent waters of the channelled river around Hari-ki-Pairi.

Split by a barrage north of Haridwar, the Ganges flows in two principal channels, divided by a long sliver of land. The main natural stream lies to the east, while the embankment of the fast-flowing canal to the west holds ghats, ashrams and buildings that seem to emerge out of the water. Non-Hindus are not allowed onto the actual Har-ki-Pairi ghat where Vishnu left his footprints in stone but the platform-like island opposite it, topped by the clocktower, provides an excellent vantage point, especially for evening worship. At dusk, the spectacular daily ceremony of Ganga Arati draws a crowd of thousands on to the islands and bridges. Lights float down the river, and priests perform elaborate choreographed movements, swinging torches in an ancient ritual to the accompaniment of gongs and music.

Near Vishnu Ghat in the centre of town, the Shri Mayadevi temple, built on a site that dates back to the eleventh century, is dedicated to a form of shakti. Further north along the Rishikesh road, the pool of Bhimgoda was gorged out by Bhima, one of the Pandava heroes of Mahabharata.

High above Haridwar, ever conspicuous on the crest of ridge the gleaming white shikhara of the Mansa

Devi temple dominates both town and valley. The temple is easily and enjoyably reached by cable car, from a base station off upper road in the heart of town, though the steep 1.5 kilometre walk is pleasant enough early in the mornings. An elaborate queuing system leads pilgrims to darshan of the main image, showing, Mansa Devi-a triple-headed image of Shakti as the goddess Durga.

Shri Dakheshwar temple, also known as Daksha Mahadev, 6 km south of Haridwar in Khankhal, is beautifully situated with large trees above a ghat. The new main temple contains a gilded image of a snake, symbolizing Shiva. Legend relates Shiva's wife Sati was so enraged when her father snubbed Shiva by failing to invite him to a sacrifice performed on this spot that she sacrificed hereself by self-immolation.

Accommodation

- Aarti, Railway Road
- Amba Niwas, Choti Sabzi Mandi, Vishnu Ghat
- GMVN Tourist Bungalow, Belwala
- Inder Kutir Guest House, Sharwan Nath Nagar
- Kailash, Shiv Murti

Jaipur

Jaipur, in Rajasthan is about 270 kilometres away from Delhi. Amber was the capital of the Kachhawa kings who trace their descent from Kush, one of the two sons of Lord Rama, the famous King of Ayodhya. In 1727, Maharaja Sawai Jai Singh II found Amber quite small and that its rocky terrain restricted expansion. So, he chose the open plains at the foot of the Kali Kho Hill, a part of the Aravali range, the oldest mountain range in India, for building a new capital. Jaipur the new capital, became the first planned city of India. Jai Singh was a proficient astronemer and well-versed with Hindu texts.

Jaipur was designed by Vidyadhar Bhattacharya, a Bengali architect, according to the Hindu treatise, Shilp Shastra. Jaipur is built in the form of a rectangle divided into blocks with roads and avenues running parallel to the sides.

Jaipur started being known as the "Pink City" firstly because of the extensive use of locally abundant pink stone and secondly because, in 1863, Jaipur dressed itself in pink to welcome Prince Albert, consort of

Queen Victoria of England. All buildings are made of stone, brick and lime, and positioned in such a direction that rooms are well lit without being subjected to the glare of the desert sun.The modern Jaipur has surpassed its earlier limits and now extends close to the very doors of the ancient capital of Amber.

Chandramahal

The central pivot of Sawai Jai Singh's city was the seven-storeyed city palace known as Chandra Mahal. The complex sprawls on over one seventh of the area in the walled city. The Jai Niwas Garden and Shri Govind Dev Temple were a part of the complex that consisted of 36 ateliers and 52 administrative departments and, "Jantar Mantar", the observatory.

"Chandra Mahal" blended classical, Mughal and traditional Rajput architectural styles, and was approched through a series of seven imposing gateways. To its west lay the Zenana Deori with its dozens of halls, temples, *raolas* and mansions for the exclusive use of the royal ladies and their personal staff. The Jai Niwas Garden, complete with fountains, water channels and reservoirs was patterned on the Mughal gardens of Kashmir.

City Palace Museum

A part of the palace houses presently, the Maharaja Sawai Man Singh II Museum with the memorabilia of the royal life of the past. The museum displays a large variety of items collected by the royal house.The items on display include interesting collections of royal dresses, jewellery, chariots, carriages, royal howdahs (elephant seats), exquisite carpets, illustrated manuscripts and miniature paintings and unique armoury and armaments that include swords and daggers with carved heads inlaid powder boxes, all in the appropriate atmosphere of a princely building.

Of the items on display, particularly striking are two silver urns, which according to the Guinnes Book of Records, are the largest silver objects in the world. These gigantic silver urns were got produced by silver smiths by Maharaja Madho Singh II for the purpose of carrying the sacred water of the river Ganga on his foreign journey, when he went to England to attend the coronation ceremony of Edward VII, in the early 20th century.

Jantar Mantar

This astronomical observatory was the brainchild of the builder of Jaipur, Maharaja Sawai Jai Singh, who built it in the 18th century. The huge instruments were used to study the movement of the constellation and the stars in the sky. Enormous sun dials still provide accurate time.

Ishwar Lat

Ishwar Lat, the tower known to local dwellers as "Swarga Suli" was constructed by Raja Ishwar Singh, one of the successors of Sawai Jai Singh, to commemorate his remarkable victory over the Marathas. The tower offers one of the most breath-taking views of the city.

Hawa Mahal

This "Palace of Winds" with its unique architecture, has made Jaipur famous throughout the world. The five-storey pryramidal building of pink sandstone, exquisitively fretted with fine screens, allowing for free play of breeze in the hot summer months was built by the poet king, Sawai Pratap Singh in 1799. The structure has 553 niches and windows, with overhanging latticed balconies.

The Palace borders one of the busiest thoroughfares of the city and was used by the royal ladies to watch the activities outside from the privacy of the balconies without being seen.

Nahargarh Fort

Cresting a hill about 600 ft. above the city, the Nahargarh Fort, also known as Sudarshangarh, was built by Jai Singh II in 1734 AD, for the defence of the city.

The walls of the fort run along the ridge and within are such architectural beauties as the Hawa Mandir and Madhvendra Bhawan. Along the ridge-top road it provides magnificent views down to the Man Sagar Lake.

Amber Fort Palace

The capital of the kachhawa kings for six centuries before the birth of Jaipur, Amber stands atop a range of craggy hills, about 10 kilometres away from the present city. The fort is remarkable as much for the majestic grandeur of its surroundings as for its sturdy battlements and beautiful palaces. The solemn dignity of its red sandstone and white marble pavilions, set alight by the setting sun on a summer eve, when reflected in the lake at the foot of the hill, is a sight be behold.

Amber is the classic romantic Rajasthan fort-palace. Its construction was started by Man Singh I in 1592 and completed by his descendant Jai Singh I. Its rugged forbidding exterior belies an inner paradise where a beautiful fusion of Mughal and Hindu styles finds its ultimate refinement.

The splendour of Amber is the result of contributions of many successive rulers. In the fort are several handsome structures. *Diwan-e-Am*, or the Hall of Public Audience, a beautifully proportioned hall open on three sides, stands on two rows of ornamented pillars. *Diwan-e-Khas*, or the Hall of Private Audience has a delicate mosaic work in glass.Sukh Mandir is guarded by sandalwood doors inlaid with ivory. Throughout the fort, finely carved lattice-windows exquisitely painted doorways and halls, and finely sculptured pillars, walls with precious stones and mirrors set into the plaster draw the attention of visitors.

At the base of the hill, in the shadow of the mighty fortifications is the temple of Garuda, the holy vehicle of Lord Vishnu. The beautifully carved gateway of the temple is flanked by large statues of elephants. A small museum neatly displays some of the archaeological finds of the area. The royal cenotaphs including a memorial to Maharaja Man Singh I, with fine carvings in bas relief depicting scenes from mythology and the famous romantic legend *Dhola-Maru* are other attractions in the vicinity.

Sheesh Mahal

Sheesh Mahal in the Amber fort is considered, by many, as the world's best Chamber of Mirrors.The clever use of mirrors adds a glowing richness to the room's motifs. So brilliant is the work in Sheesh Mahal that if a room is darkened and even a single candle lit, reflections and images glisten cheerfully all over.

Jal Mahal

This small palace is set in the middle of a small

lake—the summer resort of the royal family. A paved causeway leads upto the beautiful palace.

Jaigarh Fort

Named after Jai Singh II, the fort perched on a cliff, is surrounded by huge battlements with inside walkways offering stunning views on all sides.

Gaitor

Located fifteen kilometres from Jaipur it is here the memorial to the royal family of Jaipur, a small tribute to their contribution to the glory of the city-state, stand amidst reverential silence. The graceful *chattries,* centophs, made in white marble, are beautifully carved. The cenotaph of Maharaja Sawai Jai Singh II, the founder of Jaipur is the finest. A dazzling structure in white marble its elegant dome is supported by twenty carved pillars. Other notable structures are of those of Pratap Singh and Madho SinghII.

Galta

Twenty kilometres from Jaipur is Galta, a fine spot for a day's outing. The natural springs here are said to have curative properties. There are also several temples in the area, noteworthy among them being the temple of Sun God.

Sisodia Rani-Ka-Bagh

The charming palace and the terraced garden decorated with beautiful fountains were built by a Sisodia princess. It is profusely adorned with painted murals of hunting scenes and episodes from the Radha Krishna legends. There are two temples in the complex, one each dedicated to Lord Vishnu and Shri Hanuman.

Rambagh Lake

Rambagh Lake is another popular place and the Rajasthan Tourism Development Corporation has built cottages here, for visitors.

Accommodation

- Jaimahal Palace, Civil Lines
- Ramgarh Palace, Bhawani Singh Road
- Clarks Amer, J. Nehru Marg
- Bissau Palace, Chandpole Gate
- Khasa Kothi, Mall Road
- Lakshmi Vilas, Sawai Ram Singh Road

Jaisalmer

The westernmost town of Rajashtan, Jaisalmer is at a distance of 275 kilometres from Jodhpur and is a desert city par excellence, its honey coloured fort emerging from the flat dry sands like a fairy-tale kingdom, abounding in ancient palaces, temples and delicately sculpted houses. This is one of Rajasthan's most enchanting cities, tranquil and beautiful, its soft desert-yellow streets spiced with bright oranges, reds, yellows and blues of turbans, scarfs and skirts. As the sun sets, the sandstone buildings emit the lustrous glow that make Jaisalmer the "Golden City".

After its foundation as a Rajput stronghold by Rawal Jaisal of the Bhatti clan in 1156, a turbulent and heroic history unfolded. Initially there were constant wars with the neighbouring Rajput states of Jodhpur and Bikaner; later, in 1294, Muslim invaders attacked and conquered Jaisalmer, inducing large-scale Johar suicide by the warriors and their womenfolk, In the 14th Century the Bhatti Rajputs retook the city, but provoked a second sacking when they challenged the Muslims at Ajmer. Relations with the Muslims improved, and in 1570 the ruler of Jaisalmer married one of his daughters to Akbar. From the 17th Century the city prospered as a market centre for traders on the overland routes between India and Central Asia: the magnificent havelis of the merchants bear witness to those times.

Jaisalmer Fort

Every part of Jaisalmer fort, from its outer walls to the palace, temples and houses within, is made of soft yellow sandstone. The narrow winding streets are flanked with carved sandy facades, and from the bastions, some of which still bear cannons, you can see the thick walls that drop almost 100 m to the town below. Today the fort stands strong, housing nearly a quarter of the town's population, and strict rules limit additional buildings.

A paved road punctuated by four huge gateways winds up to the fort, built when the city was founded in 1156. The fourth gateway leads into the main chowk, which these days becomes a crowded mass of colour and life during festive celebrations, but was once the scene of the gathering of troops, marriage parties and the terrible act of johar when women chose death above dishonour for themselves and their children after their husbands left for the battlefield. The chowk is dominated by the old palace of the Maharawal, whose five-storey façade of balconies and windows display some of the finest masonry work in Jaisalmer, while the interior is painted and tiled in typical Rajput style. The monarch would address his troops and issue orders from the large ornate marble throne to the left of the palace entrance.

The temples in the fort are dedicated to Surya, Lakshmi, Ganesh, Vishnu and Shiva. Walls, ceilings and pillars bear exquisite sculpted motifs, and small corridors and stairways connect one temple to another. In a vault beneath the Sambhavnath temple, the Gyan Bhandar contains Jain manuscripts, paintings and astrological charts dating back to the eleventh century.

The Havelis

The streets of Jaisalmer are flanked with numerous honey-pale facades, covered with lattice work and floral designs, but the city's real showpieces are its havelis. Each of these extravagant mansions, comprising three or more storeys around a central courtyard, was commissioned by a wealthy merchant during the eighteenth or nineteenth century. Their stonework was the art of silavats, a community of mansons responsible for much of Jaisalmer's unique sculpture.

The large *Patwon-Ki-Haveli,* not far from Narayan Niwas in the north of town, was constructed over fifty years by the Patwa merchants, traders in brocades. Five separate suites with individual entrances facing a narrow street are connected from within, and all have flat roof areas the views are excellent. Traces of stylish wall paintings survive in some rooms.

Salim Singh's small haveli provides Jaisalmer's only favourable memory of the tyrannical Salim Singh Mohta, Prime Minister in 1800, who impoverished the citizens through vigorous taxation and extortion rackets. His curious family home is topped with small bluish domes; its upper floor, enclosed by a protruding balcony, is best from the roof of Natraj Restaurant. The house is still lived in, but you can go inside. On the road to Malka Pole, you pass the decorative façade of the late 19th Century *Nathmalji-ki-haveli,* also built for a Prime Minister of Jaisalmer. Visitors are not allowed inside the haveli.

Gadi Sagar Tank and the Folklore Museum

South of the city through an imposing triple gateway, Gadi Sagar Tank, built in 1367, was once Jaisalmer's sole water supply. Its north and east banks are flanked with ghats and temples whose sandstone bricks glow with a warm deep ochre in the evening light. This peaceful place is the focus of the festival of Gangaur in March, when women fling flowers into the lake and pray for a good husband, the Maharawal heads a procession to the tank amid a pomp and splendour unchanged for generations.

The delightful little Folklore Museum near the tank's main gate has some interesting displays of folk art, much of it religious. Locally styled wooden statues of Krishna and Radha, musical instruments, paintings and a travelling temple are among its exhibits.

Desert Festival

In January or February, depending on the lunar calendar, RTDC organizes a huge desert festival, more for the sake of tourists than out of tradition, which features camel racing, dances, music, puppet shows and moustache competitions. Accommodation is provided in a special "tourist village"

Accommodation

- Deepak Rest House, Fort
- Jaisal Castle, Fort
- Laxmi Niwas, Fort
- Flamingo, Central Market
- Jawahar Niwas Palace, Amar Sagar Road

Jammu

Jammu is approximately 600 kilometres from Delhi.

Sprawling on the banks of the River *Tawi,* surrounded by lakes, hills, temples and fortresses, Jammu is chiefly known for its multitude of temples. Everywhere in the city the skyline is pierced with the spires of temples, earning it the epithet of temple city.

Raghunath Group of Temples

Devoted to Lord Rama, the hero of epic Ramayana, work on the temple was started in 1853 by the founder of the present city; Maharaja Gulab Singh. The interior of the Raghunath Temple is covered with gold leaf. The other temples in the complex are devoted to other Hindu Gods and Godesses.

Ranbireshwar Temple

The other famous temple is the Ranbireshwar Temple, which by its sheer height, dwarfs every other building around it. Dedicated to Lord Shiva, the temple is renowned for its large crystal lingams fixed on stone slabs.

Many of the other temples also attract attention by their grandeur and the legendary past. Most of these house splendid sculptures in marble of variegated colours.

Amar Mahal Palace Museum

Amar Mahal Palace is built in the style of a French chatean. The grandeur of its setting atop a hill overlooking Tawi river far below conveys a feeling of timlessness.

The museum contains memorabilia of the royal family, and excellent collection of Pahari miniatures in addition to a portrait gallery of the fomer ruling dynasty.

Dogra Art Gallery

The gallery has a large collection of miniature paintings from the hill schools of North India, including one series from the Basohli School where ornaments have been depicted by using tiny roundels of shimmering green sequin-like objects which are actually insect wings!

Shrines Baba Budhan Shah's mazghar near the Civil Airport is a shrine dating back to the 16th Century. Other shrines worth visiting are the Gandhi Nagar Ziarat,

Pir Mitha Ziarat, and Khankan Sharif Pir Rushan Shahwali Sahib.

Bahu Fort

High on the hill, Jammu's oldest edifice Bahu Fort commands an excellent view of the city.

Picnic Spots

There are two beautiful lakes a short drive away from Jammu Tawi, Surinsar Lake, 42 kilometres away is an ideal site for a picnic, as well as for an overnight stay. Mansar Lake, 80 kilometres away is fringed by forest clad hills.

Patnitop, 112 kilometres from Jammu city on the National Highway, is cool all the year round because of the altitude, right at the very top of a hill, 2024 metres, a year round tourist destination with all facilities available.

Vaishno Devi Temple

Sixty two kilometres from Jammu, Vaishno Devi attracts tens of hundreds of pilgrims annually. Motorable road is available up to Katra, 48 kilometres away from Jammu. The remaining 14 kilometres uphill all the way, is covered on foot or on pony. The famous cave shrine is situated at an altitude of 5200 mtrs. on the slope of

Trikuta mountain. In the cave, Vaishno Devi is represented by the lithic symbols of the trinity of the Goddesses Maha Lakshmi, Maha Kali and Maha Saraswati.

The pilgrimage to the holy cave of Vaishno Devi is an enlightening experience. For the religious it is a journey of deep faith and fulfilment, while the general tourist is enthralled by the surrounding scenic splendour and the idyllic beauty of the nature. The area abound in folk stone sculptures at a number of sacred and scenic spots, viz. Pindian, Shankaracharya Hill, Deva Mai Temple, Agar Bawa Jito, Dera Baba, Banda and Shiv Kohri Cave.

Kangra

Kangra, above the valley of the Banganga and below the Dhauladhar hills, is usually just passed through by the passengers who get off trains from Pathankot or Jogindernagar on their way to Dharamsala, 18 km north. Buses from all over Kangra valley, and further east and west, pull into the bus stand 1 km north of the town centre. Before the creation of Himachal Pradesh state, Kangra was capital of a district of the same name; it fell prey for centuries to invasions of Sikhs and Muslims, before the British took control in 1847 and reinstated the Katoch rajas in the town that they had founded in the 10th Century. The precipitous Dhauladhars, the Bajreshwari Devi Temple dominates a courtyard chequered in marble and black stone. The temple's legendary wealth invited much Muslim interest between the 12th and 15th Centuries; Mahmud of Ghazni, Ferox Shah Tughluq and Sikander Lodi all took their turn sacking and looting. It was finally laid low by an earthquake in 1905; what you see today is the result of extensive rebuilding, and holds little architectural appeal. The only remaining valuable possessions are the silver parasols that shade the idol, though the site is still important to devotees of Shakti, the female embodiment of Shiva's energy.

Kangar's crumbling yet still sturdy fort, accessible by rickshaw, imperiously surveys the river valley from 4 km south. It too was damaged by the earthquake, and is a shadow of its former self, overgrown and inhabited by screeching green parrots that flit through a few simple temples still tended by priests. High gates, some British-built, span a cobbled path the deserted ramparts. It was the fort, incidentally, supposedly built over the ear of Shiva, that give the name to town and district.

Accommodation

- Ashoka Hotel, Dharamsala Raod,
- Maurya
- Hotel Anand, Nehru Bazaar.

Kausambi

Kausambi is 45 kilometres away from Allahabad, via Bamrauli.

The enormous ruins are spread through several villages. Two-Kosam-Inam and Kosam-Khiraj have names suggesting their links with the ruins of the city of Kausam. According to the epics, Kausam was founded by a descendant of the Pandavas who left Hastinapur when it was destroyed by floods from the Ganga. In the Buddha's time it was the capital of the Vatsa king, Udayana, and is one of the earliest historical cities of the region. According to Hiuen Tsang, the Buddha preached here and two viharas (monasteries) were built to commemorate the event.

The site is demarcated by the remains of a wall with bastions at regular intervals. The ramparts, which form an approximate rectangle over 6 km in perimeter still average more than 10 m above field level, while the bastions tower up to nearly 23 m. Orignally made of mud they were later surfaced with bricks. There was a moat filled with water from the Yamuna River. The town was occupied continuously from 8th Centruy BC to 6th Century AD. In the southwest corner are possibly the remains of a palace. The main stupa (5th Century BC) measured 25 m in diameter and 25 m in height. There is also the damaged shaft of a sandstone column, probably crected during the rule of the Mauryan Emperor Ashoka. Another column was removed to Allahabad Fort by the Mughals. When Kausambi was first discovered by Cunningham, coins and terracotta figurines were scattered over the surface.

Kedarnath

Kedarnath at the head of Mandakini river, is one of the most scenically located Pilgrimage Centres. The valley, about two kilometres long and half a kilometre wide is like an amphitheatre surrounded by snow-clad high mountains. This place is about 430 kilometres away from Delhi, and, approximately 200 kilometres from Rishikesh through mountain tracks. Vehicles can reach only up to a place known as Gaurikund. From here, one has to go on foot or hire a pony, to trasverse about 14 kilometres, through a narrow mountain track to reach the temple.

Kedarnath Temple

Standing in the middle of a wide plateau surrounded by lofty snow covered peaks, Kedarnath temple makes an imposing sight. A number of legends in Hindu mythology explain the divinity of Kedarnath. It was from here—the place marked by a small lake presently known as Gandhi Sarovar—it is said that Yudhistira, the eldest of the Pandava brothers of the epic Mahabharata departed to heaven. Pandavas built a temple to commemorate the death-place of their eldest brother.

The present temple, built in the 8th Century A.D. by Adi Sankaracharya stands adjacent to the site of the earlier temple. Unlike in other shiva temples, the deity here is roughly a conical rock signifying the hump of a bull, the form of which Lord Shiva was said to have taken. The body of the bull is supposed to be submerged.

Samadhi of Adi Sankaracharya

Behind the Kedarnath temple is the Samadhi of Adi Sankaracharya.

The nearest road-head to Kedarnath is Gaurikund, from where one has to trek on foot or go on a pony for about 14 kilometres on a difficult hilly track, in order to reach the temple complex.

Trijuginarayan

Some distance away from Kedarnath is this place where the wedding of Lord Shiva with Parvati was solemnised, according to legend.

Khajuraho

Khajuraho is the temple kingdom known for its creative genius from 950 AD, located at a distance of about 560 kms from Delhi, 395 kms approximately from Agra and nearly 420 kms from Varanasi. This place is located at 287 kilometres from Lucknow. The superb temples built a thousand years ago by Chandela Kings, Rajput rulers, are exceptionally well executed. Only 22 of the original 85 temples have survived the onslaught of time and destructions during invasions. A large number of temples and shrines dedicated to Gods Vishnu and Shiva and Goddesses Parvati and Kali mingle with the classic beauty of Jain temples, their spiers rising into a blue sky.

Among the finest examples of cultures and wall carvings in India, the 22 temples display an amazing assortment of stone erotica. The sculptured temple tiers depict scenes from every-day life, but, it is for the sensuous carvings of erotica and woman in all her moods that these temples have become more popular. Nymphs, maidens, buxom women and athletic men engage in explicit sexual activities. The delicay and finesse with which these sculptures have been executed have put them on par with the best art the world has to offer.

The Kandaria Mahadev temple at Khajuraho best embodies the excellence of the temple architecture for which the place has become known.

Accommodation

- Jass Oberoi, By-pass Road
- Taj Chandela, Chattarpur
- Clarks Bundela
- Khajuraho Ashok
- Jhankar
- Payal
- Lakeside
- Harmony
- Sunset View

Kota

Kota, 230 km south of Jaipur on a fertile plain fed by Rajasthan's largest river, the Chambal, have some beautiful gardens, while its old palaces house the best museum in all Rajasthan.

In the 17th Century, when Kota was declared capital of a newly independent princely state by the Mughal Emperor Jehangir, it was ruled by Rao Madho Singh of the Hadachauhan Rajputs. Today it is one of Rajasthan's major commercial and industrial cities, with hydro, atomic and thermal power stations along the banks of the Chambal, and Asia's largest fertilizer plant. The nuclear plant of Rawat Bhata, protected by stringent security 60 km southwest, is notorious for its impact on local villagers.

Greatly prized saris from the village of Kaithoon, 20 km southeast of Kota, are sold in all the markets. Made of tightly woven cotton or silk, and often highlighted with golden thread, they are known here as *Masoorie* and elsewhere as *Kota doria sari.*

The residential areas, bazaars, fort, City Palace and museum east of the Chambal face harsh buildings and factory smokestacks across the river. Kishor Sagar, an artificial lake built in 1346, gives picturesque relief. The red and white palace in its centre, Jag Mandir, was commissioned by Maharani of Mewar in 1740 and can be visited only with permission from the Superintendent Engineer of Kota. Gardens to the north of the tank are lush with viridescent mango trees, dahlias and palms. Crocodiles and gharial sun themselves in a shallow pond in the Chambal Gardens on the edge of the river a few kilometres south of the fort.

Kota's fort, raised above the flat bank of the Chambal 2 km south of the bus stand, was built in 1264 by Rajkumar Jait Singh of Bundi. In a turret of the fort wall at the main gate, the Government Museum has a small collection of clothes, weapons and miniature paintings and a fascinating hand-drawn plan of Kota's manoeuvres during the Mutiny of 1857 that shows positions of defence and attack in minute detail.

Construction of the City Palace and offices of state within the fortifications began in 1625, and continued sporadically until the early years of this century. Although the older fort ramparts are falling into disrepair, the palaces are still in excellent condition. Apartments in the heart of the palaces house the excellent Maharao Madho Singh Museum, approached through a brightly painted gateway flanked by elephants. Among a vast collection of carefully decorated weapons, the size of severity of which is almost out of this world, are spears, daggers, firearms, arrows in fine quivers and shields adorned with the solar symbol of the Hadachauhan Rajputs, large enough to protect an elephant. Solid silver artefacts and fading sepia photographs of viceroys, maharajas, polo teams and Queen Victoria record the extravagance of royalty, while the outstanding examples of Kota Kamba, miniatures from Kota's school for painting, are the best to be seen in India.

A sickening array of stuffed animals in the basement is accompained by photographs of proud hunters. The most spectacular apartment is Raj Mahal, which contains the royal throne. Its walls, decked with 18th Century paintings of the exploits of Krishna, hunting parties and Maharajas, glow with mosaics of gold and glass, while the ceiling glitters with silver and mirrors.

Accommodation

- Brijraj Bhawan Palace
- Chaman
- Chambal Tourist Bungalow
- Meghraj
- Navrang

Kullu

Kullu approximately 200 kilometres away from Shimla, may well be among the narrowest valleys in the world edged between the river Beas on one side and the towering Himalayas on the other. Shrines dot the countryside and apple orchards abound.

There are three important temples in Kullu, viz., Raghunathji Temple, built in the 17th Century; Devi Jagannathi Temple and the Bijli Mahadev Temple. The Shivling in this temple is shattered regularly by lightning which is then rebuilt by the temple priest using butter.

Basheshar Mahadev Temple, near Kullu has carved stone sculptures.

Accommodation

- Apple Valley Resorts, Mohal
- Vaishali, Gandhi Nagar
- Sarvari
- Aroma Classic, Circuit House Road

Kumbhalgarh

Kumbhalgaṛh Fort, 84 kilometres from Udaipur was the second most important fort of the Mewar Kingdom, after Chittaurgarh. Built mostly by Maharana Khumba, it is situated on a west facing ridge of the Aravallis, commanding a great strategic position on the border between the Rajput Kingdoms of Udaipur and Jodhpur. It gives superb views over the lower land to the north-west, standing over 200 m above the pass leading via Ghaneroa towards Udaipur. This is where Prithviraj died and the young Udai Singh was saved by his nurse Panna Dai.

Seven gates guarded the approaches, while seven ramparts were reinforced by semicircular bastions and towers. The 36 km-long walls were built to defy scaling while their width enabled chariots to be driven along. The walls enclose a large plateau containing the smaller Katargarh Fort, inside which has the decaying palace of Fateh Singh, a garrison, 365 temples and shrines, and a village. The occupants and the fort's dominant location enabled defenders to see aggressors approaching from a great distance. Kumbhalgarh is believed to have only been taken once and that too because the water in the ponds was poisoned by enemy Mughals during the reign of Rana Pratap.

The first gate, Arait Pol is some distance from the main fort; the area was once thick jungle harbouring tigers and wild boar. Signals would be flashed by mirror in times of emergency and danger. Hulla Pol is named after the point reached by invading Mughal armies in 1567. Hanuman Pol contains a shrine and temple. The Bhairava Pol records the 19th Century Chief Minister who was exiled. The fifth gate, the Paghra Pol is where the cavalry assembled; the Star tower nearby has walls 8m thick. The *Top-Khana* is alleged to have a secret escape tunnel. The last, Nimbu pol has the Chamundi temple beside it.

The Palace

It is a 30 minutes walk from the car park to the roof of the Maharana's Durbar Hall. Tiers of inner ramparts rise to the summit, and the appropriately named Badal Mahal or Palace in the Clouds, with the interior painted in pastel colours. The views from the palace, over the walls to the jungle-covered hill sides and across the deserts of Marwar towards Jodhpur, are stunning. The palace rooms are decorated in a 19th Century style and some have attractive coloured friezes, but are unfurnished. After the maze-like palace at Udaipur, this is very compact. The Maharana's palace has a remarkable blue Durbar Hall with floral motifs on the ceiling. Polished chunar-lime is used on walls and window sills, but the steel ceiling girders give away its late 19th century age. A gap separated the merdana palace from the zenana palace. Some of the rooms in the zenana have an attractive painted frieze with elephants, crocodiles and camels. A circular Ganesh temple is in the corner of the zenana courtyard. A striking feature of the toilets was the ventilation system which allowed fresh air into the room while the toilet was in use. The Mahadeva Temple in a gorge below contains black marble slabs inscribed with the history of Mewar.

Kumbhalgarh Wildlife Sanctuary

Mostly west of the fort, the sanctuary has enabled the endangered wolf to breed, and support leopard, sloth, chowsingha, sambar, hyena, flying squirrel, crocodiles and a variety of birds.

Accommodation

- Aodhi (Watchtower) lodge,
- PWD Rest House at Kumbhalgarh.

Kurukshetra

Kurukshetra in Haryana, about 150 kilometres from Delhi, has been the germinating ground of the essence of what we call Hinduism. The dictate to action without the hope, the wish of reward is a philosophy that has guided the Indian psyche for thousands of years. It is one of those holy towns that has borne the imprint of Lord Krishna's footsteps.

Kurukshetra is the land where Manu wrote "Manusmriti" where learned Indian sage scholars compeled the Holy Rig Veda and Sama Veda.

Mythology has it that Kurukshetra was witness to the Mahabharata battle fought between the Pandavas and the Kauravas. In the battle of Right versus Wrong, it is here, Lord Krishna who was the charioteer of Arjun delivered to the wavering Arjun, the celestial " Gita Updesh", the path of selfless "Duty", "Knowledge" and single hearted devotion.

Stanesvara Mahadev Temple at Thanesar

It was here the Pandavas prayed to Lord Shiva and received blessing for the victory in the battle of

Mahabharata.

About two kilometres from Thanesar on Kurukshetra-Pehowa Road lies a tank named Narkatari. It is here, says legends, that Bhishma Pitamah of Mahabharata epic lay on a bed of arrows.

Ban Ganga

The legends of Ban Ganga are related to the epic battle of Mahabharata. This lies about four kilometres from Kurukshetra. Legend says that Ban Ganga was created by Arjun by an arrow for quenching the thirst of Bhishma Pitamah while he was on his death bed of arrows.

Jyotisara

Jyotisara lies five kilometres from the Kurukshetra Railway Station. It retains the divinity as the birth place of the holy Bhagwat Gita. A visitor can see a banyan tree here on a raised plinth. It was under this holy banyan tree that" Lord Krishna" deliverd the doctrine of Karma and showed his celestial image of Himself as the Creator, the Protector and the Destroyer.

Accommodation

- Purakeet Motel

Kushinagar

Set against a pastoral landscape, the small hamlet of Kushinagar 53 km west of Gorakhpur, is revered as the site of the Buddh's Mahaparinirvana, his death and cremation that marked his final liberation from the cycles of death and rebirth. During the Buddha's lifetime, Kushinara, as it was then called, was a small town in the kingdom of the Mallas, surrounded by forest. It remained forgotten until the late 19th Centruy when archeologists rediscovered the site, and began excavations - based on the writings of 7th Century Chinese Pilgrims, including Hiuen Tsiang.

Set in a leafy park at the heart of Kushinagar, the Nivana Stupa, dated to the reign of Kumaragupta I (413-55 AD), was extensively rebuilt by Burmese Buddhists in 1927. Within the accompanying shrine lies a large gilded reclining Buddha, reconstructed from the remains of an earlier Malla Image, and the surrounding area is strewn with stupas erected by pious pilgrims, and the ruins of four monasteries. At a crossing immediately southwest, excavations continued at the Mathakunwar shrine, where a stunning 10th Century blue schist

Buddha has been unearthed. About 1.5 km southeast of the main site — surrounded by fields of rice, wheat and cane — the crumbling bricks of the Ramabhar Stupa are thought to be the original Mukutabandhana Stupa erected to mark the spot of the Buddha's cremation.

Today Kushinagar is rediscovering its roots as a centre for international Budhism, and is home to many viharas (monasteries), including a Tibetan Gompa devoted to Shakyamuni (the historical Buddha), a Burmese vihara, and temples from China and Japan. The strikingly simple Japanese Temple, built by the Atago Isshin World Buddhist Cultural Association, consists of a single circular chamber housing a golden image of the Buddha, softly lit through small, stained-glass windows.

Accommodation

- International Buddhist Guest House, opposite the Tibetan Gompa Pathik Niwas.

Leh

Ladakh, sometimes called "Little Tibet" is situated to the North-east of the great Himalayan divide, its limited inhabitants forming part of the Tibetan racial stock. Situated at the apex of a triangular plateau formed by the Indus, at an altitude of 11,500 ft. above sea level is Leh. Leh is the biggest oasis of the mountain region and the heart of Ladakh. Leh is located at about 300 kilometres from Srinagar, as tae crow flies.

A temple dedicated to Maitreya, the future Buddha, and the Gonkhang Temple of Guardian Divinities are important landmarks in Leh.

A smile is something you will see on each of the ten thousand inhabitants of this matchbox town.

Hemis, the biggest of monasteris [or gompas] 49 kilometres from Leh, has a valuable store of *thankas* including the biggest, displayed once every twelve years. It also contains a number of gold statues and stupas inlaid with precious stones.

On the way to Hemis is the Thikas Monastery, perched on a hill top. Known for its architectural beauty, its wall paintings are exquisite. Close by is the

7.5 metres high Buddha image in the Shey Gompa (made of copper, and plated with gold). The Spituk Monastery, eight kilometres from Leh is the proud possessor of a number of intriguing *thankas;* Icons of Buddha and the 900 years old temple of Mahakali. The face of the Goddess is uncovered only once a year for the masses.

The Alchi and Likir Gompas, are located near Saspol on the Srinagar-Leh road. They have a number of gigantic clay statues of Buddha in various forms. There are a number of very old wall paintings to be seen. Alchi Gompa was built a thousand years ago.

Also on the way to Hemis Gompa and 1.5 kilometres from Leh, is the summer palace of the erstwhile Raja of Leh. Set on hill and housing the largest golden topped Victory Stupa, the monastery has a two-storeyed statue of the sitting Buddha in copper and gold.

Possibilities are endless for trecking and climbing using Leh as a base. Among the best tracks are Leh-Kargil via Suru Valley and Leh Zanskar-Kishtwar-Manali.

Accommodation

- Galden Continental
- K-Sar (Peerless)
- Bijoo
- Kang-lha-chhen

Kargil

The other district of Ladakh is Kargil. In Kargil, one can see some of the finest examples of Turkish architecture in the form of Mosques. Some very fine hand-fretwork, beautiful designs of net in wood is also evident in a newly built mosque a few kilometres off Kargil.

Accommodation

- Highlands
- Karavan
- Tourist Bangalow, Hospital Road

Lucknow

In the approximate centre of Uttar Pradesh, 570 km east of Delhi, the state capital Lucknow is best remembered for the ordeal of its British residents during the five months siege of 1857. However, the city had earlier witnessed the last days of Muslim rule in India, before the final capitulation to the British. In fact the summary British deposition of the incompetent last Nawab of Avadh — or Oudh as the British called it — Wajid Ali Shah, is usually numbered among the root causes of the "Mutiny". Many of Lucknow fading 19th Century monuments bear the scars of the fighting, and of the destruction wrought by the British army when they eventually reagained control.

Most of Lucknow's monuments are spread along or near the southern bank of the Gomti, a sluggish weed-covered stream when the rains aren't falling. Close to the main central bridge lies the modern economic centre of Hazratganj, with the Shah Najaf Imambara to its north near the riverbank. Further west, beyond the ruins of the Residency, the road passes the majestic Bara Imambara, leading through the large gate of Rumi Darwaza to the Hussainabad Imambara. South of Hussainabad, between Hazratganj and Charbagh, the old city sector of Aminabad holds a maze of busy streets and fascinating markets.

Hazratganj

Along the river, opposite the Carlton Hotel on Rana Pratap Marg, squats the huge dome of the Shah Najaf Imambara, named after the tomb of Ali in Iraq and at its best when adorned with lights during Muharram. Its musty interior holds some incredibly garish chandeliers used in processions, several tazia, and the silver-faced tomb of the decadent and profligate Ghazi-ud-din-Haidar (1814-27), buried with three of his queens.

The Imambara was commandeered as a sepoy stronghold in 1857, and the crucial battle that enabled the British to relieve the Residency was fought in the adjacent pleasure gardens of Sikandrabagh on 16 November. It took one and a half hours of bombardment for the soldiers of Sir Colin Campbell to breach the defence of the two thousand sepoys; then the Sikhs and 93rd Highlanders poured through, to embark on a rampage of slaughter. Tranquil once again, Sikandrabagh is now home to the National Botanical Research Insitute and the beautiful Botanical Gardens, with their conservatories, nurseries, herb, rose and bougainvillaea gardens, and maincured lawns.

Close to the centre of Hazratganj, its grounds dotted with derelict Avadhi monuments, Lucknow's small zoo also serves as an amusement park with a miniature train of view the animals. Head through the zoo to reach the State Museum with the delicate, speckled-red-sandstone sculpture from the Mathura school of the Kushana and Gupta periods (first-sixth centuries AD). Besides sculpture from Gandhara, Mahoba, Nalanda and Sravasti, it boasts a gallery of terracotta and even an Egyptian mummy. Musical instruments, paintings and constumes provide atmosphere in the Avadh Gallery; while the natural history section is a taxidermists dream.

Accommodation

- Amber, Naka Hindola
- Avadh Lodge, Ram Mohan Rai Marg
- Baba Tourist Lodge, Charbagh Railway Station
- Carlton, Shah Najaf Road
- Charans, 16 Vidhan Sabha Marg

Hussainabad

In the west of the city, in the vicinity of Hardinge Bridge around old Lucknow, lie several crumbling relics of the Nawabs of Avadh. Chief among them is the Great or Bara Imambara, which boasts one of the largest vaulted halls in the world-50 metres long and 15 metres high. Flat on top, slightly arched inside, and built by Asaf-ud-Daula in 1784 without the aid of a single iron or wooden beam, the roof was constructed using a technique known as *Kara Dena,* in which bricks are broken and angled to form an interlocking section and then covered with concrete several feet thick. Adjacent to the Bara Imambara and overlooking it is Asaf-ud-Daula's Mosque, set upon a two tiered arcaded plinth with two lofty minarets.

Staddling the main road west of the main gates, the colossal Rumi Darwaza is an ornamental victory arch modelled on one of the gates to Asia Minor at Istanbul (known to the Islamic world in Byzantine times as "Rumi"). Now decaying, it sports elaborate floral patterns and a few extraordinary trumpets. Steps lead up to open chambers that command a general prospect of the monuments of Hussainabad.

A short distance further west, the lavish Hussainabad Imambara is also known as the Chota ("small") Imambara, or the Palace of Lights, thanks to its fairy-tale appearance when decorated and illuminated for special occasions. The raised tank in front of it, which is approached via a spacious courtyard, adds to the overall festive atmosphere. A central gilded dome dominates the whole ensemble, busy with minarets, small domes and arches and even a crude miniature Taj

Mahal. Built in 1837 by Muhammad Ali Shah (1837-42), party to provide famine relief through employment, the Imambara Houses a silver-faced throne, plus the tombs of important Avadhi personalities. The dummy gate opposite the main entrance was used by ceremonial musicians, while the unfinished watch-tower is known as the Satkhanda or "Seven Storeys", even though only four were ever constructed. West of the Imambara, and surrounded by ruins, are the two soaring minarets and three domes of the Jami Masjid, completed after the death of Muhammad Ali Shah which does not admit non-Muslims.

Beyond the Hussainabad Tank, east of the Hussainabad Imambara, the isolated 67 metre-high Hussainabad Clocktower, an ambitious Gothic tower completed in 1887, built by Muhammad Ali Shah to house the offices of the Hussainabad Trust, and the Picture, Gallery, also known as the Muhammad Ali Shah Art Gallery. Exhibits in its large hall include old photographs and paintings including a famous portrait of the ineffectual and feeble last Nawab of Avadh, Wajid Ali Shah (1847-56). Aurangzeb's Mosque on the high ground towards Hardinge Bridge known as Lakshman Tila was the site of Lucknow's original 15th Century settlement.

The Residency

The Residency rests in peace amid landscaped

gardens southeast of Hardinge Bridge - a battle scarred ruin left exactly as it stood when the siege was finally relieved by Sir Colin Campbell on 17 November 1857. Its shattered tower became a shrine to the tenacity of the British in India, and continued to be maintained as such even after Independence.

The pockmarked Residency itself holds a small museum. Circular steps descend into its bowels, to the huge cellar known as the *TIKHANA* where many of the women and children took shelter. On the ground floor, the Model Room, the only one with its roof intact, houses a large model of the defences and of the Residency, and a small but excellent collection of etchings and old photographs.

Several victims of the siege are buried in the cemetery next to the ruined church west of the Residency. Not far away east, along the river, the rather dull Shaheed Smarak is a corresponding post-Independence memorial to the Indian martyrs who died here fighting the British in the "First War of Independence".

Ludhiana

A very rapidly growing town, 311 kilometres from Delhi on the southern bank of the Sutlej River, Ludhiana is a major textile and light engineering centre. The rich agricultural area around it supports a large grain maket. Founded in 1480 by Lodi princes from Delhi, it subsequently passed through a number of hands. Around it at Aliwal, Ferozeshah, Mudki and Sobraon are important battle-grounds from the First Sikh War.

The fort includes the Shrine of Pir-I-Dastgir, also known as Abdul Kadir Galani. There is an annual pilgrimage of Muslims and Hindus to the Muslim Saint's tomb. There are other tombs belonging to members of Shah Shuja's family while they were in exile from Afghanistan. The town is also the home of the Christian Medical College Hospital, which along with the C.M.C. Hospital in Vellore, with which it is in partnership, is one of South Asia's major teaching and research hospitals. The world famous Punjab Agricultural University is on the edge of town. It has an excellent museum.

Accommodation

- Amaltas, G.T. Road.
- City Heart, near Railway Station
- Grewals, 148 Ferozepur Road.
- Gulmor, Ferozepur Road
- Nanda, Bhadaur House.

Manali

Beyond Kullu, Manali is a major resort in the valley located about 40 kilometres from Kullu. Set amidst largely forests of towering cedars circled by snowy peaks and the unending roar of the river Beas as a constant companion, Manali also offers unparalleled opportunities for trekking, rock climbing, angling and winter sports. Closer treks are Solang Nallah, Beas Kund and Naggar; the more serious treks are Keylong, Chandatal Lake (4,200 mt.) and across Baralacha Pass (4,800 mt.).

Tibetan Monastery : The monastery has several Budha images and *thankas.*

Vashisht Springs : The hot water sulphur springs are said to be having curative qualities.

Jagatsukh : This was the ancient capital of Kullu. There are some ancient temples here.

Solang Valley : Picnic spot, with skiing slope enroute to Kothi, with glaciers close at hand.

Fishing : The mountain streams around Manali, are ideal for angling, especially for trout.

Accommodation

- Manali Ashok, Naggar Road
- Sterling Himalaya Continental
- Pandhratan Resorts
- Ambassador Resorts
- Piccadily, The Mall
- Banon Resort, The Mall

Mandi

At the point where the southern plains meet the Kullu and Kangra valleys, 158 km north of Shimla, Mandi straddles the River Beas, its houses clinging to the rising slopes of the gorge. For centuries a trading post for Ladakhis heading south — mandi means market — it boasts few sights, through Tarna Hill, 2 km northwest of the centre, holds a fine collection of temples, built in 16th Century Nagari style and carved with a medley of deities. The gates and spire of the largest, dedicated to Bhutnatha, are lavished in gold and silver.

Accommodation

- Heritage Guest House
- Raj Mahal
- Siva, Main Road.

Mathura and Vrindavan

These two towns situated at a distance of approximately 130 kilometres from Delhi, are of very religions importance to all those who believe and worship Lord Krishna. The religious and folk lore connected with Lord Krishna are thriving reasons for the believers to visit these places. It was here Lord Krishna lived his mischievous childhood and carried out his youthful dalliances chronicled in the Indian mythology.

Visitors can see even today the prison cell in Mathura where the parents of Lord Krishna were chained and the place where He took birth in this world. Mathura, on the banks of the River *Yamuna*, has been a sacred pilgramage centre through countless centuries, and the temples and shrines that line the water-front testify to its antiquity.

The Government Museum at Mathura is a superb repository of fine sculpture, terracotta images, coins and bronze objects that date from the 5th century B.C. to the 12th century A.D.

Accommodation

- Kwality
- Madhuwan
- Modern
- Raj

Meerut

Meerut is about 65 kilometres from Delhi.

Meerut is best known as the place where the Indian Mutiny started on 10 May 1857. The British cantonment has a particularly fine Mall. The cemetery of St. John's Church (1821) contains many interesting memorials including one to Sir David Ochterlony.

Meerut was a settlement in Ashoka's time and contains various Hindu and Muslim buildings from the 11th Century onwards. The Baleshwar Nath Temple is pre-Muslim, and several other old Hindu shrines surround the Suraj Kund tank built in 1714 by Jowalbhir Mal and fed by a canal from the Ganga. The Jama Masjid (1019) was built by Mahmud of Ghazni's Wazir. Although later restored by Humayun, it is one of the oldest mosques in India. The red sandstone Shah Pir Maqbara (1628) on Hapur Road was built by the Empress Nur Jahan and further west on Delhi Road is the Abu Maqbara, with a large tank. Qutb-ud-din, Aibak is believed to have built the Maqbara of Salar Masa-ud-Ghazi (1194).

Mount Abu

Mount Abu, 192 kilometres from Udaipur is Rajasthan's only hill resort and is very popular locally; many come from Rajasthan and Gujarat to escape the heat. The hill station stretches along a 20 km long plateau and is approached from Abu Road. The shops and restaurants are clustered in the compact centre. There is attractive country side to explore as it is well wooded with flowering trees with numerous orchids during the monsoon and a good variety of birdlife.

Mount Abu, known as Nandivardhan was the home of the legendary sage Vasishtha. One day Nandini, his wish-fulfilling cow, fell into a great lake. Vasishtha requested the gods in the Himalaya to save her; so they sent Arbuda, a cobra who carried a rock on his head, dropped it into the lake, displacing the water and saving Nandini. The place became known as Arbudachala 'The Hill of Arbuda'.

Dilwara Jain Temples : 5 km from town centre and set in beautiful surroundings of mango trees and wooded hills, the temples have superb marble carvings.

The complex of five principal temples is surrounded by a high wall, dazzling white in the sunlight. There is a resthouse for pilgrims on the approach road.

Chaumukha Temple : The grey sandstone three storey building, is approached through the entrance on your left. Combining 13th and 15th Century styles, it is generally regarded as inferior to the two main temples. The colonnaded hall contains four-faced images of Tirthankara Parsvanatha, and figures of *dikpalas* and *yakshis*. Along the entrance avenue on the right is a statue of Ganesh.

Adinatha Temple : This temple lies directly ahead. Immediately outside the entrance to the Temple is a small portico known as the Hastishala built by Prithvipal in 1147-59 which contains a figure of the patron, Vimla Shah, the Chief Minister of the Solanki King, on horseback. Vimla Shah commissioned the temple dedicated to Adinatha in 1031-32. The riders on the 10 beautiful carved elephants that surround him were removed during Alauddin Khilji's reign; the damaged elephants were restored recently. Dilwara belonged to Saivite Hindus who were unwilling to part with it until Vimla Shah could prove that it had once belonged to a Jain community. In a dream the Goddess Ambika instructed him to dig under a champak tree where he found the huge image of Adinatha and so won the land. To the Southwest behind the hall, is a small shrine to Ambika.

It is an early example of the Jain style in western India, set within a rectangular court lined with small shrines and a double colonnade. The entire temple is built with white marbles. Hardly a surface is left unadorned. Makaras guard the entrance, and below them are conches. The cusped arches and ornate capitals are beautifully designed and superbly made.

As in Gujarati Hindu temples, the main hall focuses on the sanctum which contains the 2.5m image of Adinatha, the first Tirthankara. The sanctum with a pyramidal roof has a vestibule with entrances on three sides. To its east is the Mandapa, a form of octagonal nave nearly 8m in diameter. Its 6m wide dome is supported by eight slender columns; the exquisite lotus ceiling carved from a single block of marble rises in "concentric circles carved with elaborately repeated figures. Superimposed across the lower rings are 16 brackets carved in the form of the goddesses of knowledge.

Risah Deo Temple, opposite the Vimala Visahi, is unfinished. It encloses a huge brass Tirthankara image weighing 4.3 tonnes and made of panchadhatu—gold, silver, copper, brass and zinc. The temple was commenced in the late 13th Century by Brahma Shah, the Mewari Maharana Pratap's Cheif Minister. Building activity was curtailed by war with Gujarat and never completed.

Luna Vasihi or Neninatha Temple to the north of Adinatha Temple, was erected by two wealthy merchnats Vastupala and Tejapala, and dedicated to the 22nd Tirthankara; they also built a similar temple at Girnar. The attractive niches on either side of the entrance were for their wives. The small domes in front of the shrine containing the bejewelled Neminatha figure, the exquisitely carved lotus on the sabhamandapa ceiling and the sculptures on the colonnades are especially noteworthy.

Trevor's Tank, 50 m beyond the Dilwara Jain temples is the small nature reserve based around Trevor's Tank. Crocodiles laze on the banks and a variety of animals come to drink at dawn and dusk. There are superb views from the trails that lead through the Park.

Adhar Devi, 3 km from town, is a 15th Century Durga temple carved out of a rock and approached by 220 steep steps. There are very good views.

Sunset Point, Nakki Lake and Honeymoon Point : Sunset Point and Honeymoon Point give superb views across the plains to the west. They can both be reached by a pleasant walk from the bus stand, about 2 km. The route to Honeymoon Point goes past the Nakki Lake.

The Headquarters of the Spiritual University movement is Om Shanti Bhavan with its ostentatious entrance on Subhash Road, which runs yoga courses, with the Spiritual Museum near the horse stand.

Art Museum and Gallery, Raj Bhavan Road: Small collection which includes some textiles and stone sculptures.

Accommodation

- Connaught House, Rajendra Marg
- Hillock, Opp. Petrol Pump
- Hilltone, Near Bus Stand
- Abu International, Opp. Polo Ground
- Aravalli

Mussoorie

This is a self-styled queen of hills, about 235 kms. from Delhi, spread out over 15 kms. along a horseshoe-shaped ridge.

Off this runs a series of buttress-like subsidiaries. It is an extremely popular destination among Indian tourists especially as it is the nearest hill station to Delhi. The credit for its establishment goes to a Captain Young who built the first British residence in 1826 (in Landour). At the eastern end of town, a narrow spur leads to Landour (2,270m) and the old barracks area. The winding road through the crowded Bazaar leads up to the site of Capt. Young's large house. There are lovely walks, and the extra 300 m height above Mussoorie here appears to offer cleaner, pine scented air.

To the west is Convent Hill and Happy Valley where Tibetan refugees have settled and the pleasant Municipal Garden. Mall road connects Kulri and Library Bazars. Like other hill stations, Mussoorie is best for walks. Lal Tibba and nearby Childe's Lodge on the highest hill is 5 km from the Tourist Office. There is a 400 m ropeway to Gun Hill (so called because prior to

Independence, a mid-day gun fire enabled residents to set their watches!). This can be reached by bridle path also from the Kutchery on The Mall. The view of the snow capped peaks is stunning and best at sunrise. The Camel's Back Road starts from Kulri and ends at Library and is a very pleasant 3 km walk with the Camel's Rock enroute.

Kempty Falls, 15 km on the Chakrata road, is pretty and a popular picnic spot.

Accommodation:

- Dunsvirk Court, Vincent Hill, Upper Road, Baroda Estate.
- President (Jaypee), Barlow Ganj.
- Padmini Nivas, Library, The Mall.
- YWCA Holiday Home, The Mall.

Nainital

The dramatic lake of Nainital, set in a mountain hollow at an altitude of 1938 metres, 277 km north of Delhi, gives its name to the largest and most important town in Kumaun. Discovered for Europeans in 1841 by Mr. Barron, a wealthy sugar merchant, Nainital swiftly became a popular escape from the summer heat of the lowlands, and continues to be one of India's main hill stations. Throughout the year, and especially between March and July, hordes of tourists and honeymooners pack the Mall, the promenade that links Mallital (head of the lake), the older colonial part of Nainital at the north end, with Tallital (foot of the lake).

Nainital's position within striking range of the inner Himalayas—visible from vantage points above town—makes it a good base for exploring Kumaun. Corbett National Park, Almora and Ranikhet are all within easy access. When the town's commercialism gets a bit too much, it's always possible to escape into the beautiful surrounding country to lakes such as Sat Tal, where the foothills begin their sudden drop towards the plains to the south, or to the forested ridges around Kilbury.

Accommodation

- Tourist Bangalow, Sat Tal
- Naini Retreat
- Everest

Palampur

Palampur is located at about 30 kilometres from Dharamshala.

Tea gardens carpet the hills, pine and deodar forest cloak them, no wonder Palampur is restfully green, a quiet resort that has still to be discovered by the tourist.

Baijnath

Located at about 13 kilometres from Palampur is a Shiva temple dedicated to Shiva Vaidyanath (Lord of Physicians). This is supposed to be the temple where Ravana worshipped Shiva to gain immortality. The Baijnath Temple is considered to be one of the twelve "Jyotirlingas".

Billing

This place is said to be amongst the finest of sites for hand gliding in the world.

Accommodation

- Mansad
- Silver Oaks Resort
- Palace Motel

Patiala

Patiala, 249 kilometres from Delhi was once the capital of an independent state, along with Jind and Nabha, whose ruling houses were all Sikh. It suffered at the hands of the European adventurer, George Thomas and was later consolidated into the Sikh Empire of Ranjit Singh, who included it in treaty arrangements made with the British in 1809. Thereafter, the Maharaja remained loyal to the British.

The most impressive building in this well-kept town is the huge concentric fort, the creation of Maharaja Ala Singh in the late 18th Century. Surrounded by a moat, it is 8km to the north east of town on the Chandigarh road. Bahadurgarh is a good example of a *Nara Durg,* a large fort built on a plain and capable of housing a garrison large enough to repulse strong attacks such as the unsuccessful but nevertheless fierce Maratha attempt in 1794. It looks majestic from the air and is now surrounded by intensively cultivated fields.

The Old Motibagh Palace in the town is perhaps one of the largest homes in Asia. The rambling central building is surrounded by lawns and trees. A combination of European, Rajput and Mughal styles, part of it is now the National Institute for Sports. There are 15 dining halls and many outbuildings. The Sheesh Mahal has a Museum and Art Gallery. The collection includes ethnography, arms, natural history and miniature paintings.

Accommodation

1. Green, Mall Road

Pinjore

Known in Aryan times as *Panchpura,* the walled Yadavindra Gardens at *Pinjore*, 22 km north of Chandigarh on the Shimla Road, is one of many sites associated with the exile of the Pandavas, chronicled in the Mahabharata. The well-watered beauty spot, at the foot of the Shivalik Hills 4 km south of Kalka, originally belonged to the rajas of Sirmaur. Under the Moghuls, it was taken over by Aurangzeb's foster brother, Fidai Khan, who erected three pleasure palaces for his wife amid the cypress trees and lush maidans. Legend has it that the Raja reclaimed his summer retreat by sending a female fruit-seller with goitre as a present to the imposters. On being told that the woman's unsightly swelling was caused by the local water, the Begum and her entourage fled.

The walled gardens harbour a small otter sanctuary, aviary, and zoo, and are popular picnic spots. One of three attractive Moghul summer palaces has been converted by Haryana Tourism into a hotel and is a convenient place to break a car journey between Delhi and Shimla.

Accommodation

- Budgerigar, Yadavindra Gardens

Pushkar

Pushkar lies in a narrow dry valley 11 kilometres from Ajmer overshadowed by the impressive rocky hills. There are spectacular views of the desert at sunset from the hills around the village.

For most of the year Pushkar is a gentle and peaceful lakeside village on the edge of the desert, though it has been transformed by the year-round presence of large numbers of foreign tourists, it is still a good place to rest for a few days.

Pushkar lake is one of India's most sacred. Ghats lead down to the water to enable pilgrims to bathe. Fa Hien, the Chinese traveller who visited Pushkar in the 5th Century AD commented on the number of pilgrims. However, though several of the older temples were subsequently destroyed by Aurangzeb, many remain. The only Brahma temple in the country, at the farther end of the lake, is believed to have sprung from a lotus flower dropped by Brahma. It is a particularly holy shrine since it is believed to mark the spot where Brahma was incarnated. Pilgrims still come throughout the year.

Cattle Fair

Kartik Poornima (full moon) in November is marked by India's greatest cattle and camel fair. The huge cattle and camel fair is Pushkar's biggest draw. Over two lakh visitors and pilgrims and hordes of cattle and camels with their semi-nomadic tribal drivers, crowd into the town. Farmers, breeders and camel traders buy and sell. Sales in leather whips, bits, shoes, embroidered animal covers soar, while women bargain over bangles, clothes, pots, necklaces of glass beads from Nagaur, ivory work from Merta and printed cloth from Jodhpur and Ajmer.

There are horse and camel races on all days and betting is heavy. The Ladhu Umt is a race in which teams of up to 10 men will cling to the camel, and one another in a hilarious and often chaotic spectacle. There are also sideshows of jugglers, acrobats, magicians and folk dancing. At nighfall, there is music and dancing outside the tents, around friendly fires. Pilgrims bathe in the lake, the night of the full moon being the most auspicious time, and launch boats of marigold and rose petals in the moonlight.

Accommodation

- Peacock Holiday Resort
- Pushkar Palace
- Sarovar, Near Ajmer Bus Stand
- Everest Guest House, Near Marwar Bus Stand
- Oasis, Near Ajmer Bus Stand

Rajaji National Park

Around 830 square kilometres of the Himalayan foothills immediately east of Haridwar are taken up by Rajaji National Park, which belongs to the same forest belt as Corbett National Park, 180km east. Although not geared for tourism to the same extent as Corbett, the park is absolutely beautiful, with a similar range of wildlife most notably elephants, but also tigers, even a rare species of ant-eaters.

The main gates of the national park are at Chila, 13 km east of Haridwar by road, across the Ganges. The visitors don't have to go into the core area to experience the jungles of Rajaji. It is also possible to venture in from Rishikesh, or from the road between the two, paralleling the canal that marks the western boundary of the huge fringe forest.

Hemkund and the Valley of Flowers

Starting from the hamlet of Govind Ghat, 28 km south of Badrinath on the road to Joshimath (local buses will stop on request), an important pilgrim trail winds for 21 steep kilometres up to the snow-melt lake of Hemkund (4328m). In the Sikh Holy book, the Guru Granth Sahib Govind Singh recalled meditating at a lake surrounded by seven high mountains; only this century was Hemkund discovered to be that lake. A large gurudwara (Sikh temple), and a small shrine to Lakshmana, the brother of Rama of Ramayana fame, now stand alongside.

An alternative trail forks left from Ghangaria, climbing 5 km to the mountain bugyals of the Bhyundar valley- the Valley of the Flowers. Starting at an altitude of 3352m, the valley was discovered by the visionary mountaineer, Frank Smythe, in 1931, who named it, not surprisingly, on account of its multitude of rare plants and beautiful flowers. The meadows are at their best towards the end of the monsoons, in early September; they too have suffered at the hands (or rather feet) of large numbers of visitors, and camping is not allowed here either. As a result it is not possible to explore the ten-kilometre valley in its entirety in the space of a day's hike from Ghangaria.

Rampur

This town located at 189 kilometres from Delhi was founded in 1623 by Shah Alam and Hussain Khan, two Afghan Rohillas who had sought service with the Mughals. Under Shah Alam's grandson, Ali Muhammad Khan, the Rohillas were united in what was to become known as Rohilkhand, and later expanded their empire to Almora in the North and Etawah in the South. On the death of Najib-ud-daula in 1772 the region was invaded by the Marathas. With the Nawab in Oudh's and British support the Marathas were beaten off, but afterwards the Rohillas fell foul of Oudh and in the ensuing Rohilla War (1773-4) the empire was lost and later dismantled. The Nawab of Rampur remained loyal to the British during the Mutiny and supported them in the 2nd Afghan War, and was rewarded with a grant of new territory.

There is an extensive palace and fort. The State library has oriental manuscripts and an excellent collection of 16th-18th centuries portraits including a contemporary painting of Babur and a small book of Turki verse with notes by both Babur and Shah Jahan.

Accommodation

- Modipur
- Tourist Bungalow

Ranthambore National Park

Ranthambore a tiger resort located at a distance of about 165 kilometres from Jaipur is dominated by the conspicuous Vindhyan hill range with its steep escarpments. The bed layers of the sedimentary limestone and sandstone rocks are clearly visible, lying one over the other. The geological formations and low rainfall are responsible for its dry deciduous vegetation. At first sight, the dhok and salar forests, leafless for the greater part of the year, hardly seem to be a habitat fit for a large predator like the tiger. But, a closer look reveals that the primary producers, vegetation (acacia and zozyphus species) and grasses are of rich forage value for herbivores. Well-distributed water points, some perennial lakes like Padam Talab, Rajbagh, Gilaysagar and river pools like Bhakola and Kamaldhar complement the excellent habitat.

Accommodation

- Ankur Resort
- Castle Jhoomar Baori
- Hunting Lodge
- Kamadhenu

Rishikesh

Rishikesh is 238 km northeast of Delhi and 24 km north of Haridwar, at the point where the wooded mountains of Garhwal rise abruptly from the low valley floor, and the Ganges crashes onto the plains. Its many ashrams continue to draw devotees and followers of all sorts of seird and wonderful gurus, with the largest Shivananada Ashram, in particular, renowned as a yoga centre.

Confusingly, the name Rishikesh is applied to a loose association of five distinct sections, encompassing not only the town but also hamlets and settlements on both sides of the river,—Rishikesh itself the commercial and communications hub; sprawling suburban Muni-Ki-Reti; Shivananda Nagar just north; the multi-storeyed and multi-coloured temple of Lakshmanjhula, staddling the river a little further north; and the assorted ashrams around Swarg Ashram on the east bank.

Most of the pilgrims who pass through Rishikesh on their way to the Himalayan shrines of the Char Dham pause for a dip and puja at the large sandy expanse of Triveni Ghat, close to the centre of town.

The ghat looks especially spectacular during arati (evening worship), when *DIYA* lights float on the river. Nearby, at Bharat Mandir, Rishikesh's oldest temple, a black stone image of Vishnu is supposed to have been consecrated by Adi Shankara in the 9th Century; the event is commemorated during Basant Panchami, to mark the first day of spring.

The dense-knit complex of cafes, shops and ashrams collectively known as Swarg Ashram, opposite Shivananda Nagar, is the most attractive part of Rishikesh, backing on to forest-covered hills where caves are still inhabited by sadhus. The Swarg Ashram itself, popularly referred to as *Kale Kumbli Wale,* was founded in honour of Swami Vishudhanand, who came here in 1884 and habitually wore a black (*kala*) blanket (*Kumble*). The most conspicuous of the other ashram-temples is Parmarth Niketan, whose large courtyard is crammed with brightly-clad gods and goddesses. Gita Bhavan runs a free Ayurvedic dispensary here, as well as selling books and khadi, handloom cloth.

Around 2 km north of Swarg Ashram, a path skirts the east bank of the river, and beautiful sandy beaches sheltered by large boulders, en route to Lakshmanjhula. A footbridge named after the brother of Ram spans the river here as it negotiates its final rocky course out of the mountains.

Accommodation

- Arvind Lodge, Yatra Bus Stand
- Banprast Ashram
- Baseraa, 1 Ghat Road
- Bhandari Swiss Cottage, Lakshmanjhula
- Ganga Kinar, Barrage Road

Samode

Samode, 42 km northwest of Jaipur on the outskirts of Shekawati but normally visited as a day trip from the city, is notable for a superb restored eighteenth-century palace with exquisite murals and delicate stonework. The centre of attention here is the main hall, Sheesh Mahal, or mirror palace, where the glasswork is even more stunning than at Amber. The Samode Palace is now a heritage hotel, and its highly priced rooms offers the chance of luxurious stop enroute to Shekawati.

Samode Fort and Samode Bagh are the two more attractions for the tourists.

Accommodation

- Samode Palace
- Luxury Tents

Saranath

Twelve kilometres from the sacred city of Varanasi is Saranath which is of importance to Buddhist pilgrims. The famous Deer Park here marks the remote and tranquil spot where the Buddha preached his first sermon. It was here that Buddha first journeyed following his enlightenment in search of his five disciples. The area reveals many of the excavated sites of buildings belonging to the early years of Buddhist history.

Sariska Tiger Reserve

In the semi-arid zone of Rajasthan, there are two excellent faunal areas, Sariska and Ranthambore; both tiger reserves. A regular hunting lodge has been converted into a Hotel, in Sariska. This place is located about 175 kilometres from Agra an approximately 100 kilometres from Jaipur.

The Aravallis are the oldest mountain range of India, running from Mt. Abu in the south-west to Delhi in the north-east. The Sariska reserve is part of the northern half, about 200 kilometres, south of Delhi. It is an undulating terrain of low hills, steep escarpments, wide valleys and hill plateaus consisting of a complex geology of ingeneous, metamorphosed and sedimentary hill ranges. Rainfall is low, the average being 600 mm during the monsoon season, July, August and September. The semi-arid vegetation is stunted dry deciduous, with a mixture of thorny species. The forests are dominated by salar on the higher and steep slopes, dhok on the lower slopes of the hills and zizyphus, acacias, dhak, grewia and capparis in the valleys. Grasses grow abundantly in open patches on hills as well as in the valleys. There are evergreen glades of Jamun, Kadam,

Khajur, Ficus and Rohini in the hill-folds and along streams and pools in the lower reaches of the hills.

Sariska's wildlife includes the tiger, panther, deer and antelope.

Accommodation

- Kushalgarh Palace
- Sariska Palace
- Tiger Den Tourist Bungalow
- Forest Rest House

Shekawati

Beyond the last ripples of the Aravalli range, about 63 kilometres north of Jaipur, lies the easternmost extent of the Thar desert, where small towns rest between sand dunes and infertile expanses of dusty land in the area known as Shekawati. While the terrain is barren, dry and hostile, the architecture and painting of the region's buildings possess a beauty and richness unparalleled in all India. Mansions, palaces and cenotaphs in a succession of sleepy, semi-rural towns are decorated inside and out with detailed and vivid scenes of folk tales, religious stories, local merchants and cities, animals, local customs and even Eruopeans with their Victorian technology, each mural bordered with delightful floral designs. Most of the towns are so small that you can amble at whim without losing your bearings, and be sure of finding rich rewards on any path you follow.

As Shekawati has not yet become part of the well-trodden tourist trail in Rajasthan few locals speak English, and there's little prospect of accommodation or western food. The region presents great scope for exploration. Only the main towns have been listed here, but-perhaps with the help of Ilay Cooper's Guide to Painted Towns of Shekawati, produced locally by Shri Om Printers in Jhunjhunu, you should be able to find exciting sites in any town or village you pass through. Many of the buildings are still privately owned; ask permission to enter any house, and respect the custom of removing your shoes before you do so.

The first people to settle in the lands north of Jaipur, Muslims of the Khaimkani clan, established two small states based at Jhunjhunu and Fatehpur in 1450. Their hold on the region was broken in 1730, when the Rajput Sardul Singh of the Shekawat clan took over Jhunjhunu. Two years later he consolidated Shekawati rule by helping his brother to seize Fatehpur from its Muslim Nawab.

Although the area is known as Shekawati, the Shekawat Rajputs were only responsible for the construction of the forts in each town. The caravan route known as the "spice road" passed through the region on its way between China and the coast of Gujarat, and it was the local merchants – the Marwaris, Hindus of the Vaisya caste, and Jains–who funded the building and painting of family houses, temples, wells and rest houses. During the 19th Century–when the development of new ports and increased brigandry damaged overland trade, many Marwaris moved with British encouragement to Bombay, Madras and, especially, Calcutta. They continued, however, to send their profits back to Shekawati, erecting elaborate buildings either to prove their worth as prospective bridegrooms, or simply as aid projects during times of famine.

When the British left India a number of Marwaris purchased British industries, and such names as Birla and Poddar remain prominent in business today. However, many merchant families have now left Shekawati and settled more permanently in the major urban centres. The region's current inhabitants continue to rear goats and sheep for their wool, and reap what they can from the dry earth, while maintaining the traditional crafts: tie-and dye, screen printing, lacquer work, wood carving and silverwork.

Travelling to Shekawati from Jaipur, your most likely point of arrival is Sikar, two hours journey by road or almost twice that by train. Although Sikar has many attractive buildings, it has now extended beyond the old city walls and lost much of its original charm. With only basic lodging available, it's best to limit your stay to a couple of hours and head northwest to Nawalgarh, where you'll find better hotels and a more relaxed, rural atmosphere.

From Bikaner to the west, a four or five hour journey brings you to Fatehpur, which has some fair accommodation and is a convenient base for visiting the other Shekawati towns.

Shimla

Shimla, in Himachal Pradesh, is about 370 kilometres from Delhi.

Mountain peaks encircle the summer seat of the British empire and Shimla still retains its past historic splendours. It is everything that it was in its good old days. Wooden bungalows with gardens in which gladioli and hydrangea bloom; leisurely moments of horse riding, golf and cricket; a prominent promenade where vacationers spend time at what was once know as Scandal Point. Modern Shimla is as enchanting as ever, with its trails and forest walks, its malls and hotels, skating rinks, and fireside chats.

The Mall is Shimla's principal promenade and is best for a leisurely walk. Though it has many beautiful British bungalows, the Viceregal Lodge is really magnificent. Walks to Jakhu Hill, Summer Hill, Chadwick Falls and Prospect Hill, are really refreshing. Taradevi Temple, Sankat Mochan and Tibetan Monastery are havens of tranquility.

Kurfi

Kurfi is a picnic spot that offers excellent skiing on its slopes in winters, located quite near to Shimla.

Narkanda

This is another excellent skiing base where splendid scopes spread out invitingly for the skier.

Accommodation

- Woodville Palace, Raj Bhawan Road
- Eastbourne, Khillini
- Asia The Dawn, Mahavir Ghat
- Holiday Home, Circular Road
- Honeymoon Inn, The Mall
- Harsha, The Mall

Srinagar

Srinagar, approximately 900 kilometres from Delhi is the winter capital of Jammu and Kashmir. An ancient city, it is said to have been founded by Ashoka, the great Buddhist emperor.

Dal Lake, Nagin Lake and Anchar Lake and the River Jhelum form a sparkling network of waterways, in Srinagar. Jhelum flows gently through the centre of the city, the entire area of which is dotted by temples and shrines with nine bridges linking the two portions.

Srinagar is surrounded by low hills, and is made up of the clamour of quaint old bazaars, elegant parks and boulevards of modern Srinagar, and secluded stretches of rice fields and orchards which bring the countryside into the city.

Hari Parbat

In the middle of the city is a small but, commanding hill called the Hari Parbat. The fort was built by an Afghan Governor in the 18th Century. Crowning of the hill was done by Emperor Akbar later, with a fort, which though in ruins, is still an impressive structure. Over the ages, the sides of the hill have provided sites for many Hindu temples, Muslim Zuarats, and a Sikh Gurdwara; a wonderful sight of secularism in Kashmir.

Shankaracharya Hill

The historic Shiva temple atop the Shankaracharya Hill is an impressive feature of Srinagar. This is one of the earliest built and is the finest example of Hindu architecture in medieval times.

Mosque Hazratbal

This domed mosque made of white marble is quite famous because it enshrines a sacred hair of the Prophet Mohammed. The holy relic was brought to Srinagar by Khwaja Noor-ud-Din from Bijapur, in 1700 AD. On specific dates in a year, the holy relic is shown to the faithfuls who gather in the mosque in thousands.

Dal Lake

The Dal Lake is an enchanting silver blue sheet of water dotted with brightly coloured Shikaras (gondola-like boats) and elegant houseboats. It is the throbbing heart of Srinagar, an equatic plaza with vendors sitting in Shikaras selling all sorts of wares. Around the Dal Lake are the colourful terraced Mughal gardens, Shalimar, Nishat and Chashma Shahi, laid by the beauty loving, Mughal emperors. Magnificent chinar trees in large groups in these Mughal gardens are feasts to the eyes. Srinagar's thousands or so houseboats are moored along sections of Dal Lake, Nagin Lake and Jhelum river each decorated fancifully and named whimsically.

Shalimar Garden

Described as the "Versailles of Mughal Emperors", the Shalimar Bagh was laid out by Jahangir, with its beautiful terraces, marble pavilions, fountains and cascades. The papier-mach work on the ceiling of the central pavilion has stood for nearly 400 years.

Nishat Bagh

The Nishat Bagh (the garden of pleasure) which rises from the Dal Lake against a background of blue mountains, has inimitable charm; its terraced flower beds and water cascades enhance its splendour.

Chashma Shahi

Chashma Shahi is a beautiful garden which commands a grand view of the Dal Lake. It has a spring from which it derives the name the "Royal Spring". The water from the spring is accredited with medicinal properties.

Nasim Bagh

To the west of the Dal Lake, opposite Nishat Bagh, is the Nasim Bagh (garden of cool breezes) which was laid by Akbar, the great Mughal emperor, in a dense chinar grove.

Old City

Srinagar's old city sprawls outwards from the base of the Hari Parbat Hill. Crammed on either side of the river Jhelum, the old city is a labyrinth of sights and sounds, unlikely to be encountered anywhere else.

Khir Bhawani

About 25 kilometres from Srinagar is the shrine of Khir-Bhawani, built over a spring which mysteriously changes colour, where thousands of Hindu pilgrimes flock. The road to this shrine passes though Ganderbal famous for willow work.

Accmmodation

- Adhoo's Residency Road
- Tourist Reception Centre, Maulana Azad Road
- Grand, Sherwani Road
- Tourist Bungalow, Nagin Lake
- Tourist Hotel

Sultanpur Bird Sanctuary

Sultanpur, about 46 kilometres from Delhi on Delhi-Jaipur highway, has a Bird Sanctuary which is an attraction for the visitors. Hundreds of species of migratory birds are winged here to stay. Over 100 species have been identified. Birds from Siberia, Geese from Europe, darters, egrets, spovellers, gadwell, greylag geese etc., can be seen here.

The sanctuary's main attraction is the arrival of its water visitors. Ducks, geese, pelicans, flamingos, cormorants, sandpipers, demoiselle cranes, white ibis, spoonbills and a host of other warerbirds start settling in by the late September and arrivals continue till December.

Accommodation

- Rosy Pelican Complex

Udaipur

Udaipur is located 405 km from Jaipur, 275 km from Jodhpur and 274 km from Ajmer.

Set in the Girwa Valley amidst the Aravalli hills of Southern Rajasthan, Udaipur is a beautiful city, regarded by many Indians and foreign visitors as one of the most romantic in India. In contrast to some of its desert neighbours it presents an enchanting image of white marble palaces, placid blue lakes and green hills that keep the wilderness at bay. It is an oasis of colour in a stark and arid region.

The City of Sunrise

The legendary Ranas of Mewar who traced their ancestry back to the Sun, first ruled the region from their 7th Century stronghold Chittaurgarh. In 1586, Maharana Udai Singh founded a new capital on the shores of Lake Pichola and named it Udaipur, the 'abode of Udai' or 'the city of sunrise'. On the advice of an ascetic who interrupted his rabbit hunt, Udai Singh built a temple above the lake and then his palace around it.

Fort Palaces

Udaipur is a traditionally planned walled city, its bastioned rampart walls pierced by five massive gates, each studded with iron spikes as protection against enemy war elephants. High on the hill overlooking the lake stands the masive palace of the Maharanas, probably the largest in Rajasthan. From its rooftop gardens and balconies, you can look out over the Pichola Lake, with the Jag Niwas Summer Palace, 'adrift like a snowflake' in its centre. Around the lake, the houses and temples of the old city stretch out in a pale honeycomb.

The Old City was built in the 17th Century on undulating ground, and surrounded by a large wall with five main gates; Hathi Pol, Kishan Gate, Delhi Pol, Chand Pol and the Suraj Pol. The western side of the town is bounded by the beautiful Pichola Lake and the eastern and northern sides by moats. To the south is the fortified hill of Eklingigarh. The main street leads from the Hathi Pol to the City Palace which stands on a low ridge overlooking the **Lake Pichola.** This actually comprises a number of palaces that despite variations in design and ornamentation are intergrated into an impressive whole. It is built on a massive scale, with a blend of Rajput and Mughal influences.

The **old city** is a maze of narrow winding lanes flanked by tall whitewashed houses with doorways, decorated with Mewar folk art, windows, with stained glass or *JALI* screens, majestic *HAVELIS* with spacious inner courtyards and shops. Many of the houses within the city were given by the Maharana to retainers - barbers, priests, and artisans. Many rural landholders titled jagirdars, had a townhouse conveniently located near the palace. One of the grandest of these is the Bagor Ki Haveli, all glass work and a succession of cool shady courtyards which is the West Zone Cultural Centre.

The **Jagdish Mandir,** 150 m north of the palace, was built by Maharana Jagat Singh. The temple is a fine example of the Nagari style. A shrine with a brass Gardua stands outside and stone elephants flank the entrance steps. Inside the temple within is a black stone image of Vishnu as Jagannath, the Lord of the Universe.

City Palace

The entrance to its vast plaster façade is through the Bari Pol under which the rulers were weighed against gold and silver on their birthdays, which was then distributed to the poor. Beyond the Tripolia the Ganesh Deori Gate leads south to the fine Rai Angan, adjoined on the eastern side by the Jewel Room. From here you can wander through a number of palace enclosures, some beautifully decorated, all comparatively small and picturesque. Here and there are pretty views over the city or the lake. At the far end is the Queen's

Palace, now exhibiting palanquins, *howdahs* and photos of British Residents in a quite open atmosphere. The Chhoti Chitra Shali has interesting blue tiles and the Manak Mahal with a central garden, has been filled with figures of porcelain and glass. The Moti Mahal is decorated with mirrors and the Chini Ki Chitra Mahal has fine ornamentation of Dutch and Chinese-made tiles counterpointed with mirror work. The Bari Mahal or Amar Vilas has a pleasant garden.

On the western side of the Tripolia are the Karan Vilas and Khush Mahal, a pleasure palace for European guests with a 'grotesque mixture of European, Rajput and Mughal detailing', whilst to the south lies the Shambhu Niwas Palace. Maharana Fateh Singh added the Shiv Niwas Palace to this. Now a small hotel, one room has crystal furniture.

Museums : Half of the City Palace is still occupied by the royal family and is not accessible. There is a Palace Museum in the 'open' part, with some beautiful views across the lake. It includes the Mor Chowk, with its beautiful late 19th Century peacock mosaics. There is also armour worn by Pratap Singh, narrative wall paintings, royal cradles, toys etc. The Government Museum within the palace complex has a good collection of exhibits which include a stuffed kangaroo and Siamese twin deer.

Lake Pichola : Fringed with hills, gardens, palaces, ghats and temples, Lake Pichola is the scenic focus of Udaipur. Set in it are the Jag Niwas and the Jag Mandir Palaces. The Jag Mandir in the south is notable for the Gul Mahal, a domed pavilion built during the reign of Karan Singh. Prince Khurram, lived on this island when he was in revolt against his father Jahangir. Refugee European ladies and childern were also given sanctuary there by Maharana Sarap Singh during the Mutiny. It is now abandoned.

The Lake Palace : The Jag Niwas island to the north has the older Dilaram and Bari Mahal Palaces. They were built by Maharana Jagat Singh II in 1754 and cover the whole island.

The Jal Burj is on the water's edge, south of the town. A pleasant walk past the Jal Burj Caffe leads to the gardens of the wall with good views; a pleasant place to relax.

Other sights within the City

The Fateh Sagar Lake, north of Lake Pichola, was constructed in 1678 during the reign of Maharana Jai Singh and modified by Maharana Fateh Singh. There is a pleasant lakeside drive along the eastern bank. The Nehru Park with a restaurant and the West Zone Cultural Centre are here.

Pratap Samak : Overlooking the Fateh Sagar is the Moti Magri on which is a statue of Maharana Pratap on his famous horse Chetak. Local guides claim that he jumped an abyss of extraordinary width in the heat of the battle even after losing one leg! The path to the top winds through some attractive gardens.

Sahelion Ki Bari Gardens : This 'Garden of the Maids of Honour' is a small ornamental pleasure garden in the north of the city and contains an elegant lotus pool, gushing fountains, beautiful black marble kiosks on the corners of the pool and stunning bougainvilleas covering the walls of the enclosure. In what was a pavilion opposite the entrance is small 'children's museum' which has a curious collection of exhibits.

Ahar : 3 km east of the city are the remains of the ancient city which contains some *Chhattris* and a small museum. The *Chhattris* are in the Jain style and set on high plinths in the Mahasati. The museum contains pottery sherds and terracotta toys dating from the first Millennium BC and exhibits from subsequent periods. In the vicinity are the temples of Mira Bai and Mahavira. Nearby is the village of Ahar.

Museums

Bharatiya Lok Kala Museum, charged with the preservation of Rajasthani folk arts, has an interesting collection including dresses, dolls, masks, musical instruments, paintings and puppets. Evening puppet show and folk dancing are features here.

Zone Cultural Centre and Village on Fateh Sagar : A village created with huts from Rajasthan, Gujarat, Maharashtra and Goa faithfully replicated with a collection of colourful folk art.

Accommodation

- Lake Palace, Pichola Lake
- Laxmi Vilas Palace
- Shiv Niwas
- Shikarbadi, Govardhan Vilas, Ahmadabad R.
- Chandralok, Saheli Marg.

Nathdwara (48km) is a centre of the Krishna worshipping community of Gujarati merchants who are followers of Vallabhacharya. Non-Hindus are not allowed inside the temple containing a black marble Krishna image, but the outside has interesting paintings. Bazaar sells temple hangings illustrating the Krishna legend which originated here. These are painted on cloth with natural colours and are popular with pilgrims.

Varanasi

Varanasi is located at a distance of 800 kilometres approximately from Delhi about 600 kilometres from Agra, nearly 440 kilometres from Khajuraho.

Believed to be the oldest living city in the world, with a recorded history dating back to 2500 years, Varanasi, also known as Kashi has always been the most important centre of pilgrimage for Hindus. This place is regarded as the centre of world; the city of Gods—especially of Lord Shiva—the city of birth and death and is believed to be blessed with a special dispensation that ages back to the origin of civilisation.

A dip in the holy waters of Ganga at Kashi is considered to be capable of removing sins and awarding peace of mind. Hindu pilgrims believe that offering prayers and performing religious rites at Ganga in Kashi result in obtaining salvation to the souls of their dead relations.

One of the most pilgrim circuits is to walk along the 'Panchkrosh Road', and thus 'circle the world'. Along this pilgrim route which may take five days to cover on foot, there are as many as 108 pilgrim shrines.

A number of Hindu pilgrims come and settle down in Kashi, after discarding all their worldly belongings, attachments, pursuits etc, with the sole objective of achieving salvation of the soul by dying there. For those who cannot afford to be at Kashi at the time of death, salvation of souls is considered to be possible by immersement of the mortal remains in the holy waters of Ganga, at Kashi.

Accommodation

- Clarks Varanasi, The Mall
- Taj Ganges, Nadesar Palace Ground
- Ideal Tops, The Mall
- Baradari, Maidagin
- Bombay International, Sonarpura

Yamunaotri

In the shadow of the 6,315 mt. high Bandarpunch mountain, Yamunotri, the source of River Yamuna, is one of the four most important pilgrimages, collectively called "Char Dham", of the Garhwal Himalayas. The premier attraction of Yamunotri is the temple devoted to Goddess Yamuna and the holy thermal springs. This place is about 360 kilometres from Delhi, and approximately 130 kilometres from Rishikesh, through mountain tracks. Vehicles can go only up to a place known as Hanuman Chatti. Thereafter, are has to traverse on foot or on a pony, about 13 kilometres of a very rough, and very narrow mountain track in order to reach the temple.

Temple of Yamuna: The temple was built by Maharani Gularia of Jaipur in the 19th century.

Surya Kund: There are a number of thermal springs in the vicinity of the temple which flow into a number of pools.

Divya Shila : It is a rock pillar which is worshipped before entering the Yamunotri temple.

Commonly Followed Routes

ROUTE A

- Delhi
- Surajkund
- Sultanpur Bird Sanctury
- Meerut
- Haridwar
- Dehradun
- Mussorie
- Rajajee National Park
- Rishikesh
- Hemkund & Valley of Flowers

ROUTE B

- Badrinath
- Kedarnath
- Gangotri
- Yamnaotri

ROUTE C

- Almora
- Nainital
- Corbett National Park
- Rampur
- Mathura & Vrindavan
- Agra
- Sariska(Tiger Reserve)
- Ranthambor(Tiger Reserve)
- Lucknow

ROUTE D

- Khajuraho
- Dudhwa National Park
- Allahabad
- Kausambi
- Varanasi
- Sarnath

- Kushinagar

ROUTE E

- Jaipur
- Samode
- Shekhawati
- Ajmer
- Pushkar
- Kota
- Chittorgarh
- Jaisalmer
- Bikaner
- Udaipur
- Kumbhalgarh
- Mountabu

ROUTE F

- Panipat
- Kurukshetra
- Ambala
- Patiala
- Chandigarh
- Pinjor
- Ludhiana
- Amritsar
- Anandpur Saheb

ROUTE G

- Kangra
- Simla
- Mandi
- Kullu
- Manali
- Dalhousie
- Dharamshala
- Palampur
- Chamba
- Jammu
- Anantnag
- Srinagar
- Gulmarg
- Leh